Instant Immersion™

Spanish

developed by Mary March, M.A.

written by Jenny Lona, Ph.D.

© 2003 Topics Entertainment, Inc.

1600 S.W. 43rd Street, Renton, WA 98055 U.S.A.

www.topics-ent.com

Instant Immersion™

developed by Mary March, M.A.
written by Jenny Lona, Ph.D.

ISBN 1-59150-308-6

Edited by AOLTI
Creative Director: Tricia Vander Leest
Illustrations by Elizabeth Haidle
Art Director: Paul Haidle
Design by Paul Haidle
Maps by Lonely Planet®

Printed on 100% recycled paper. Printed in the U.S.A.

TABLE OF CONTENTS

INTRODUCTION

Bienvenido (welcome) to *Instant Immersion Spanish*™! An understanding of other cultures is critical in becoming part of a larger global community. Knowing how to communicate in other languages is one way to facilitate this process, and you have chosen a truly global language to learn. There are diverse Spanish-speaking cultures in Europe, Central and South America and the Caribbean, having a worldwide influence on cuisine, fashion, dance, theatre, architecture, and arts. Of course, there are also many Spanish-speaking communities in the United States.

Now let's get down to learning some Spanish. Did you know a large percentage of English vocabulary has roots in Latin? Spanish gets a majority of its vocabulary from Latin, so there are many similar words between the two languages. This means you already know the meaning of many Spanish words such as: *radio, problema, policía, concierto, televisión, posible, restaurante, música, banana, bicicleta, hospital, diciembre, especial,* and many more! You just have to learn the pronunciation. (As you'll see, Spanish pronunciation isn't very difficult *(difícil)*!)

This book will help you learn the basics of communicating in Spanish in a way that will be fun and easy for you. We include many popular phrases and expressions and show you how these are used in real life through example conversations and stories. Our book also provides an easy pronunciation system that will give you the confidence you need to speak Spanish. A wide range of interesting and valuable topics give you a firm grounding in the language, including how to order food like a local, how to travel comfortably within the country, even what to do when things go 'wrong'.

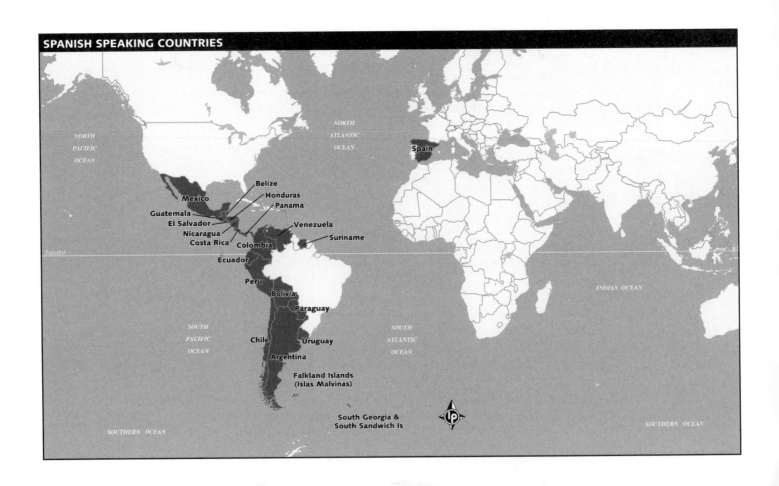

PRONUNCIATION GUIDE

Spanish is very consistent in its pronunciation, meaning that vowels and consonants (or combinations of letters) are pronounced in the same way no matter which word they appear in*. Spanish has many of the same sounds found in English, plus some special sounds you might not be used to hearing. The following chart will help you pronounce words in Spanish; throughout this book, the pronunciation of most new words is given for you, with the stressed syllable in capital letters.

Spanish vowels and consonants		Approximate equivalent in English	notation in pronunciation key
a	a	long "a" as in "bar"	(a),(ah)
b	be	like English "b" but softer; don't close your lips all the way	(b)
c	ce	before a,o,u: [k]; before e,i: [s] (or in some places, [th] as in "three")	(k),(s)
ch	che	as in "church"	(ch)
d	de	softer than English "d"; more like "th" in "then"	(d),(th)
e	e	like "a" in "take" but shorter	(eh)
f	efe	like English "f"	(f)
g	ge	before a,o,u: [g] (as in "girl"); before e,i: like "h" in "help", but stronger	(g),(h)
h	hache	ALWAYS silent	
i	i	Like "ee" as in "feet", but shorter	(ee)
j	jota	like "h" in "help", but stronger (expel more air to make the sound louder)	(h)
k	ka	like English "k" ("k" doesn't occur in native Spanish words)	((k))
l	ele	like English "l"	(l)
ll	elle	like "y" in "yes" (in some places like "j" in "jam")	(y)
m	eme	like English "m"	(m)
n	ene	like English "n"	(n)
ñ	eñe	a "nyuh" sound, like you hear in "onion" or "union"	(ny)
o	o	like English "o" in "phone" but shorter	(o),(oh)
p	pe	like English "p" (but expelling less air)	(p)
q	cu	like English "k"; always followed by "u" but the "u" is silent	(k)
r	ere	usually like "dd" in "ladder"; at the beginning of a word or between vowels, "r" makes a rolled "rrr" sound	(r),(rr)
rr	erre	a rolled "rrr" sound	(rr)
s	ese	like English "s"	(s)
t	te	like English "t" (but expelling less air)	(t)
u	u	like "oo" in "moon", but shorter	(oo)
v	ve	see "b" above; the two letters are pronounced exactly alike	(b)
w	doble ve	like English "w" ("w" doesn't occur in native Spanish words)	((w))
x	equis	generally [ks] (as in "ax"), occasionally a strong "h" sound (see "j")	(ks),(h)
y	i griega	see the possible pronunciations of "ll" above; "y" has the same	(y)
z	zeta	variation like English "s" (or in some places, [th] as in "three")	(s)
ai/ay		These combinations are always pronounced like the English word "eye".	(ai), (ay)

Although word stress is indicated for you in this book, there are three simple rules that can help you figure out where the stress falls on any Spanish word:

1. If the word ends **in a vowel, n,** or **s,** stress the next-to-last syllable.
2. If the word ends in **a consonant other than n** or **s,** stress the last syllable.
3. **Any exception to rules one and two has a written accent over the stressed vowel.**

*The one exception is "x" which is pronounced like a strong "h" in some Native American words.

CHAPTER 1

(BWEHnos DEEas)
¡Buenos días!
Good morning!

Instant Immersion Spanish™ has 16 chapters. You can work through the book chapter by chapter or skip around to the topics that most interest you. Study the expressions and vocabulary before reading the dialog or story. Say them out loud to practice your pronunciation. Read through the dialog or story as many times as you need to. Then read it out loud. Do the exercises, and check your answers in the Answer Key at the back of the book. Finally, get in a Spanish mood! Put up posters of Spanish-speaking places, enjoy your favorite Spanish or Latin American foods, listen to some Flamenco or Salsa, whatever it takes…. And have fun learning Spanish!

(meh da iGWAL)
Me da igual.
I don't care.

(BAmos)
Vamos.
Let's go.

(OHMbre)
hombre
man

(ehl)
él
he

(maNYAna)
mañana
morning

(EHya)
ella
she

(mooHAIR)
mujer
woman

(aBLAR)
hablar
to speak

(KCOmo ehsTA oosTETH)
¿Cómo está usted?
How are you?

(toMAR)
tomar
to take

(eer)
ir
to go

(oosTETH)
usted
you

(KYEHreh)
quiere
want

(ehsTOY beeEHN)
Estoy bien.
I'm fine.

(kcoMEHR)
comer
to eat

(alMWEHRso)
almuerzo
lunch

(SEHna)
cena
dinner

(dehsaYOOno)
desayuno
breakfast

DIALOG

(ehs maNYAna OOna mooHEHR) (ehLEHna) (ee oon OHMbre) (PAblo) (HABlan)
Es mañana. Una mujer (Elena) y un hombre (Pablo) hablan.
it is   a   and a

(BWEHnos DEEas, PAblo) (KOmo ehsTA oosTETH)
Elena: "Buenos días,   Pablo. ¿Cómo está usted?"

(BWEHnos DEEas ehLEHna ehsTOY beeEhn ee oosTETH)
Pablo: "Buenos días, Elena. Estoy bien. Y usted?

(ehsTOY beeEhn) (DOHNdeh KYEHreh oosTETH)
Elena: "Estoy bien. ¿Dónde quiere usted
where
toMAR ehl dehsaYOOno?)
tomar el desayuno?"
the

(meh da iGWAL) (PohDEHmos eer al kaFEH ehn ehl ohTEL)
Paul: "Me da igual. Podemos ir al café en el hotel.
we can   to the

KYEHro koMEHR oon pan DOOLseh)
Quiero comer un pan dulce."
I want

(yo tamBYEHN. EhnTOHNsehs, BA mos.)
Lise: "Yo también.   Entonces, ¡vamos!"
I   too   then

PRACTICE

Fill in the blanks using the words below.

desayuno	cena	quiere	tomar
almuerzo	dónde	usted	dónde

1. ¿ _____ quiere usted tomar la _____ ? (8 p.m.)

2. ¿Dónde _____ _____ tomar el _____ ? (8 a.m.)

3. ¿Dónde quiere usted _____ el _____ ? (12 p.m.)

4. ¿ _____ quiere usted comer?

MATCHING

Match the sentence with the picture.

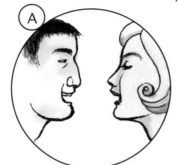

A

B

C

D

E

F

_____ 1. Una mujer y un hombre hablan.

_____ 2. Yo también. Entonces, ¡vamos!

_____ 3. Me da igual.

_____ 4. Es mañana.

_____ 5. ¿Dónde quiere Ud. tomar el desayuno?

_____ 6. Quiero comer.

FOCUS: SUBJECT PRONOUNS

SINGULAR

(yo)
yo (I)

(too)
tú (you, singular, familiar)

(oosTETH)
usted/Ud. (you, sing., formal)

(ehl)
él (he/ it, masculine)

(EHya)
ella (she/ it, feminine)

PLURAL

(noSOtrohs)
nosotros/as (we)

(voSOtrohs)
vosotros/as (y'all, plural, familiar)

(oosTEthehs)
ustedes/Uds. (you (all), pl., formal)

(EHyos)
ellos (they, m.)

(EHyas)
ellas (they, f)

VERB CONJUGATIONS

COMER
to eat

(KOmo oon POHko)
Como un poco.
I eat a little.

(koMEHmos)
Comemos mucho.
We eat a lot.

(KOmehs KARneh)
Comes carne.
You eat meat.

(koMEHYS ehspaGEHTees)
Coméis espaguetis.
Y'all eat pasta.

(KOmeh)   (KOcheh)
Ella come en el coche.
in the car

(KOmehn)   (PLAHya)
Ellas comen en la playa.
the beach

(PLAHya)
Él come en la playa.
the beach

(KOmehn)   (KAma)
Ellos comen en la cama.
in the bed

As you can see, there are four different ways to express "you" in Spanish. The familiar forms are used with children, close friends and family; the formal forms are used in other situations. In Latin America, the *vosotros* form is not used. Instead, *ustedes* is used as the plural "you" in both formal and informal situations.

Both the *nosotros* and *vosotros* pronouns have feminine forms (*nosotras* and *vosotras*) which are used only when all of the persons referenced by the pronoun are female.

Most often, subject pronouns are actually omitted in Spanish; the subject can be inferred from the verb form. For instance, "I am eating pizza" would typically be *Como pizza*, without the pronoun *yo*. Subject pronouns are included only where necessary for clarification or emphasis.

VERB CONJUGATIONS

To conjugate a verb in Spanish, remove the final two letters of the infinitive before adding the conjugated endings. You've just seen an example of a regular "-er" verb, *comer*. Here is an example of a regular "-ar" verb, **tomar**. Many other "regular" verbs have the same endings as these two verbs. (You will learn more about this process in lesson 5.)

(tohMAR)
TOMAR
to take

tomo	*(TOmo)*	*I take*
tomas	*(TOmas)*	*you take*
toma	*(TOma)*	*he/she/it/you (Ud). takes*
tomamos	*(toMAmos)*	*we take*
tomáis	*(toMAHYS)*	*y'all take*
toman	*(TOman)*	*they/you (Uds.) take*

Vamos a tomar desayuno.
We're going to have breakfast.

(trehn)
Tomo el tren.
I'm taking the train.

(KYEHrehs)   *(TRAgo)*
¿Quieres tomar un trago?
Do you want to have a drink?

¿Uds. toman café?
Do you (all) drink coffee?

CHAPTER 2

(TEHNgo AHMbreh)
¡Tengo hambre!
I'm hungry!

Reading in Spanish will help you learn how to understand the language. It is an easy, effective way to increase your vocabulary and knowledge of grammatical structures. Practice saying the idioms and vocabulary words. Study the meaning of each. Then read the story silently, trying to understand it. Read the story again out loud, focusing on the pronunciation of the words.

(keh SWEHRteh)
¡Qué suerte!
What luck!

(TEHNgo AHMbreh)
Tengo hambre.
I'm hungry.

VOCABULARY

(EHNtra)
entra
enters/ is entering

(SAleh)
sale
leaves/ is leaving

(kohnTEHNtoh)
contento
happy

(TREESteh)
triste
sad

(aMEEgahs)
amigas
friends

(KEHso)
queso
cheese

(da)
da
gives/ is giving

NUMBERS

If you want to understand a room number, tell someone your phone number, or understand how much something costs that you are considering buying, you need numbers. Try to memorize the numbers 0–10 now (Practice counting throughout the day!) and more numbers will be introduced in later chapters.

0	1	2	3	4	5
(SEHro) cero	*(OOno)* uno	*(dohs)* dos	*(trehs)* tres	*(KWAHtro)* cuatro	*(SEENko)* cinco

6	7	8	9	10
(sehys) seis	*(SYEHteh)* siete	*(Ocho)* ocho	*(NWEHveh)* nueve	*(dyehs)* diez

PRACTICE

Write the answers to these simple arithmetic problems in words.

1. tres + uno = _____

2. seis + cuatro = _____

3. dos + tres = _____

4. ocho - cinco = _____

5. nueve - ocho = _____

6. diez - tres = _____

7. cuatro x dos = _____

8. tres x tres = _____

STORY

(soo) *(HOOlya)(ehsTAHN)*
Ana y su amiga Julia están en un restaurante.
her *are*

(SAHNDweech)
Ana come un sandwich de queso.
of

(TYEHNeh)
Julia tiene dos sandwiches de queso.
has *two*

(hwahn) *(rehstahwRAHNteh)* *(leh prehSEHNta)*
Juan entra en el restaurante. Ana le presenta Juan a
to her

(MOOcho GOOSto) *(DEEseh)*
Julia. "Mucho gusto, Julia," dice Juan.
"Pleased to meet you, Julia," says Juan.

(prehGOONta) *(see)*
Entonces Ana le pregunta a Juan si tiene
to him *asks* *if he's*

hambre. "Sí, ¡tengo hambre!" dice él.
hungry *yes*

Julia le da un sandwich.   "Gracias. ¡Qué suerte!" responde
thanks

(ehsTA mooy)
Juan. Está muy contento.
He is very happy

PRACTICE

The statements below are all false. Change each one to make it true.

1. Ana y su amiga comen en el coche. _____

2. Julia tiene tres sandwiches. _____

3. Juan sale del restaurante. _____

4. Juan está triste. _____

VERB FOCUS

(ehsTAR)
ESTAR
to be

(ehsTAmos kohnTEHNtos)
Estamos contentos
We are happy.

(ehsTOY TREESteh)
Estoy triste.
I am sad.

(ehsTAS)
Estás contento.
You are happy.

(ehsTAHYS)
Estáis tristes.
You all are sad.

(ehsTA)
Está contenta.
She is happy.

(ehsTA)
Está triste.
He is sad.

(ehsTAHN)
Están contentos.
They are happy.

There are two Spanish verbs which are translated as "to be" in English. *Estar* is used to express locations and conditions of people and things, while *ser* is used to identify people and things and talk about their characteristics. Both of these verbs are irregular in the present tense.

The full conjugation of *ser* will appear in chapter 3.

CHAPTER 3

(pehrDOHN)
¡Perdón!
I'm sorry! Excuse me!

If you are traveling to a foreign country, there will be many opportunities for you to start a conversation with native speakers of the language. Don't be shy! Of course some people will be in a hurry or won't want to talk to you. However, many people will be interested to meet someone traveling in their country. You'll want to learn some basic questions and appropriate responses as well as some useful expressions.

(TEHNgo seth)
Tengo sed.
I'm thirsty.

(TEHNgo SWEHnyo)
Tengo sueño.
I'm sleepy.

(ehsTA byehn)
Está bien.
It's okay.

VOCABULARY

(ehlehsTAdo)
el estado
the state

(see)
sí
yes

(deh)
de
from/of

(DOHNdeh)
¿dónde?
where?

(AHblah)
habla
speaks

(oon POHko)
un poco
a little

(mehYAmo)
me llamo
my name is

(aKEE ehsTA)
aquí está
here is

USEFUL EXPRESSIONS

Here are some ways to say yes and no:

¡Sí!
Yes!

¡No!
No!

(KLAHro keh see)
¡Claro que sí!
Certainly!

(por sooPWEHStoh)
¡Por supuesto!
Of course!

(al kohnTRAryo)
¡Claro que no!
Of course not!

¡Al contrario!
On the contrary!

Sí, por favor.
Yes, please.

No, gracias.
No, thank you.

Sometimes bumping into people by accident can lead to introductions and even friendships. Read what Dan and Elena have to say to each other after they bump into each other in a doorway.

Dan Duncan: man   **Elena Suárez:** woman   **Inés:** girl   **David:** boy

1 | **Dan:** ¡Perdón!   **Elena:** Está bien.

2 | **Dan:** *(ehspaNYOHla)* ¿Es usted española?   **Elena:** ¡Sí! ¿De dónde es usted?
    Are you Spanish?

Dan: Soy de Seattle, Washington.
(KOmo sehYAHma)
Me llamo Dan Duncan. ¿Y Ud.? ¿Cómo se llama?
What is your name? Lit: How are you called?

3 | *(ehLEHna SWArehs)*
Elena: Me llamo Elena Suárez. Mucho gusto.

(eegwalMEHNteh)   *(mee Eeha eeNEHS)*
Dan: Igualmente.   **Elena:** Le presento a mi hija, Inés.
likewise   *This is my daughter, Inés.*

4 | *(Ohla)*   *(KWANtohs AHnyos TYEHnehs)*
Dan: Hola, Inés. ¿Cuántos años tienes?
Hi, Inés. How old are you? Lit: How many years do you have?

Inés: Tengo ocho años.
I'm eight years old.

5 | *(EHSteh ehs mee EEho)*   *(ehspaNYOHL)*
Dan: Éste es mi hijo, David. Habla un poco de español.
This is my son, David.   *Spanish (language)*

Elena: Hola, David. ¿Cuántos años tienes tú?

6 | **David:** Tengo cinco y tengo sed y tengo sueño.

PRACTICE

Study the dialog. Then, see if you can write the missing question. The response is given.

1. ¿ _____ ?   Tengo ocho.

2. ¿ _____ ?   Soy de Seattle.

3. ¿ _____ ?   Me llamo Inés.

4. ¿ _____ ?   Sí, soy española.

¿ASKING QUESTIONS IN SPANISH?

A. The easiest way to ask a question in Spanish is to simply raise your voice at the end of a sentence.

¿Ud. es mexicano?

¿Y Ud.?

¿Tienes hijos?

B. Another way is to invert the subject and the verb. (Put the pronoun or noun after the verb.) Of course, this only applies when the subject or pronoun is included.

¿De dónde es Ud.?

¿Cómo se llama tu hija?

¿Cuántos años tienes (tú)?

These are the most common ways to form questions in Spanish.

Now practice asking questions. Write a question using the method indicated (A or B), putting the words in the correct order.

Ex: inglés/habla/Ud.   (A) ¿Ud. habla inglés?

1. es/ americano/Ud.   (B) ¿ _____ ?

2. hambre/tienes   (A) ¿ _____ ?

3. hambre/vosotros/tenéis   (A) ¿ _____ ?

4. son/de dónde/Uds.   (B) ¿ _____ ?

5. carne/comes/tú   (A) ¿ _____ ?

6. tú/cuántos años/tienes   (B) ¿ _____ ?

soy	*(soy)*	*I am*
eres	*(EHrehs)*	*you are*
es	*(ehs)*	*he/she/it/you (Uds). is*
somos	*(SOmos)*	*we are*
sois	*(soys)*	*y'all are*
son	*(sohn)*	*they/you (Uds.) are*

Recall that *ser* is used to identify people and things and talk about their characteristics, as in these examples:

(soy mehheeKAHno)
Soy mexicano.
I'm Mexican.

(EHrehs eentehleeHENteh)
Eres inteligente.
You're intelligent.

(EHya ehs mee EEha)
Ella es mi hija.
She is my daughter.

(ehloTEHL ehs GRAHNdeh)
El hotel es grande.
The hotel is large.

Llamar is one of many regular –ar verbs, which means "to call". In this chapter you learned some forms of the related verb *llamarse*, "to call oneself" or "to be called". This verb is often used to ask or give someone's name. The verb *llamarse* is what's known as a "reflexive" verb; the subject of the verb and its object are the same individual(s). When you see "*se*" on the end of a Spanish infinitive verb, it is an indication that the verb is reflexive. In English, a verb is made "reflexive" by using it with a special object pronoun which is reflexive. The reflexive object pronouns of English are words like myself, yourself, herself, themselves, etc. When you use one of these pronouns, you choose the one that matches whatever the subject is.

Spanish also has a special set of reflexive object pronouns. As in English, the choice of which reflexive object pronoun to use depends on who the subject of the verb is. The Spanish reflexive object pronouns have very short forms, and they are placed directly <u>in front of</u> the conjugated verb form (rather than behind it, as is the case in English). This is what a reflexive verb looks like when it's conjugated; note the different forms of the reflexive object pronouns for different subjects:

LLAMARSE
to call oneself / be called

me llamo	*(meh YAHmo)*	*I call myself*
te llamas	*(teh YAHmas)*	*you (tú) call yourself*
se llama	*(seh YAHma)*	*you (Ud.) call yourself*
se llama	*(seh YAHma)*	*he/she/it calls him/her/itself*
nos llamamos	*(nos yaMAHmos)*	*we call ourselves*
os llamáis	*(os yahMAIS)*	*y'all call yourselves*
se llaman	*(seh YAHman)*	*you (Uds.) call yourselves*
se llaman	*(seh YAHman)*	*they call themselves*

There are many reflexive verbs in Spanish. Watch for them!

CHAPTER 4

(KWANtoh KWEStah)
¿Cuánto cuesta?
How much is it?

VOCABULARY

(keh)
qué
what

(PEHro)
pero
but

(BAHleh)
¡Vale!
OK!

(KYEHro)
quiero
I want

(ahKEE)
aquí
here

(LEHNtaMEHNteh)
lentamente
slowly

VERBS

(kohmPREHNdoh)
comprendo
I understand

(keeSYEHrah(n))
quisiera(n)
would like

BE POLITE

(MOOchas GRAHsyas)
Muchas gracias.
Thank you very much.

(aDYOHS)
¡Adiós!
Good bye!

(deh NAHda)
De nada.
You're welcome.

(por fahBOR)
Por favor.
Please.

No, gracias.
No, thank you.

(no ay deh keh)
No hay de que.
Don't mention it.

You may also want to use these words to address people in more formal situations:

(sehNYOR)
Señor /Sr.
Sir or Mr.

(sehNYOra)
Señora/Sra.
Ma'am or Mrs.

(sehnyoREEta)
Señorita /Srta.
Miss

Use these in the same way you would their English equivalents. A group of men and women can be addressed with the masculine plural, *Señores*.

NEGATION

It's easy to make a sentence negative in Spanish. Just place the word "no" before the conjugated verb. If the verb has any object pronouns, "no" will precede them, but nothing else can occur between "no" and the verb. Here are some examples:

No me llamo Nancy.
My name is not Nancy.

No comprendo.
I don't understand.

No como carne.
I don't eat meat.

No lo comprendo.
I don't understand it.

STORY

(dehpehnDYEHNteh)   *(sehÑOHrehs)*
Dependiente: Buenos días, Señores.
  clerk

Carmen: Buenos días.

John: Buenos días, Señora.

Dependiente: ¿Qué quisieran Uds.?

                                        (pahn) (eentehGRAL)
Carmen: Yo quisiera un pan integral,
                               a loaf of wheat bread

              por favor.

Dependiente: ¿Y Ud., Señor? ¿Qué quisiera?

John: No comprendo. Hable más lentamente,
                                 more
     por favor.

Dependiente: Vale. ¿Qué quisiera Ud.?

          (booÑWEHlos deh mahnSAHna)
John: Quiero dos buñuelos de manzana, por favor.
         apple fritters

Dependiente: Aquí están.
Here they are.

Carmen: *(ay AHgwa meenehRAL)*
¿Hay agua mineral?
Is there any mineral water?

Dependiente: Por supuesto, Señorita. Aquí está.

Carmen: Gracias. ¿Cuánto cuesta?

Dependiente: Tres Euros, por favor.

Carmen: Aquí están tres Euros.

Dependiente: Gracias, Señorita.

Carmen: Gracias a Ud. Adiós.

Dependiente: Adiós, Señores.

DO YOU UNDERSTAND?

Read the previous dialog carefully and see if you can answer these questions. Check your answers in the back of the book.

1. Who is *española* in this dialog? _____

2. Why doesn't John understand? _____

3. What does John want to buy? _____

4. Who asks for mineral water? _____

5. Where does this scene take place? _____

VERBS

STEM-CHANGING VERBS

"Stem-changing" verbs are Spanish verbs that have regular endings in their conjugated forms, but have an irregularity in the stem, or root, of the verb. (This is the part of the verb remaining after the infinitive ending is removed; for example the stem of *hablar* is *habl,* the stem of *tener* is *ten,* etc.) When the last vowel of the stem of one of these verbs occurs in a stressed syllable, it undergoes a change. So, the change happens in all forms of the present tense of the verb <u>except</u> *nosotros* and *vosotros.* The verb *costar,* meaning "to cost", has one common type of stem-change: from "o" to "ue". Here is the present tense conjugation of *costar:*

COSTAR (UE)
to cost

c<u>ue</u>sto	(KWEHSto)	*I cost*
c<u>ue</u>stas	(KWEHStas)	*you cost*
c<u>ue</u>sta	(KWEHSta)	*he/she/it/you (Ud). costs*
costamos	(kosTAmos)	*we cost*
costáis	(kosTAYS)	*y'all cost*
c<u>ue</u>stan	(KWEHStan)	*they/you (Uds.) cost*

When using the dictionary, you can tell a stem-changing verb by the vowel "change", usually indicated in parentheses after the verb. Another very common stem change is from "e" to "ie"; *querer* is a verb you've already seen that has that type of stem change. Here is the present tense conjugation of *querer:*

QUERER (IE)
to want / to love

qu<u>ie</u>ro	(KYEHro)	*I want*
qu<u>ie</u>res	(KYEHrehs)	*you want*
qu<u>ie</u>re	(KYEHreh)	*he/she/it/you (Ud). wants*
queremos	(kehREmos)	*we want*
queréis	(kehREYS)	*y'all want*
qu<u>ie</u>ren	(KYEHrehn)	*they/you (Uds.) want*

LOS NÚMEROS 11 - 22

11	12	13	14	15	16
(OHNse)	*(DOHse)*	*(TREHse)*	*(kahTORse)*	*(KEENse)*	*(dyehseeSEHYS)*
once	doce	trece	catorce	quince	dieciséis

17	18	19	20	21	22
dyehseeSYEHte)	*(dyehseeOcho)*	*(dyehseeNWEHve)*	*(BEHYNte)*	*(behynteeOOno)*	*(behynteeDOHS)*
diecisiete	dieciocho	diecinueve	veinte	veintiuno	veintidós

In the following exercise, write the numbers in words, just for practice. Review numbers 1–10 in Chapter 2 if you need to. Say the numbers out loud as you write them. Then, practice saying each sentence with *por favor* at the end. For example: *Quisiera dos buñuelos de manzana, por favor. Quisiera* is the polite-imperfect subjunctive form of the verb "to want" and is commonly used, but it's always good to say "please", *por favor* at the beginning or end of the sentence too.

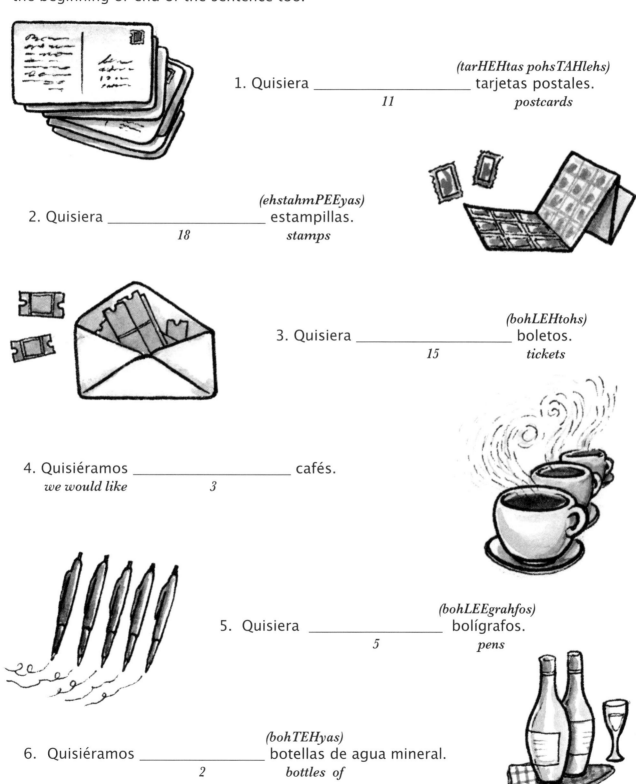

1. Quisiera _____ tarjetas postales.
                11   *postcards*
(tarHEHtas pohsTAHlehs)

2. Quisiera _____ estampillas.
                18   *stamps*
(ehstahmPEEyas)

3. Quisiera _____ boletos.
                15   *tickets*
(bohLEHtohs)

4. Quisiéramos _____ cafés.
   we would like   *3*

5. Quisiera _____ bolígrafos.
                5   *pens*
(bohLEEgrahfos)

6. Quisiéramos _____ botellas de agua mineral.
                2   *bottles of*
(bohTEHyas)

CHAPTER 5

¿Qué día es?
What day is it?

(abooRREEdoh)
estar aburrido/a
to be bored

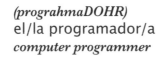

(ehl aMOHR ah preeMEHra BEESta)
el amor a primera vista
love at first sight

(koLEHreeko)
ser colérico/a
to be quick-tempered

(grahSYOHsa)
gracioso/a
humorous

(prograhmaDOHR)
el/la programador/a
computer programmer

(mooHEHR deh nehGOsyos)
la mujer de negocios
businesswoman

(seemPAHteeko)
simpático/a
nice

(ehl traBAho)
el trabajo
work

(la KAsa)
la casa
house

(ehl KOcheh)
el coche
car

(los Ohos)
los ojos
eyes

(ehsTREHya)
estrella
star

FOCUS : VERBS

(beeBEER)
VIVIR
to live

viv**o**	*(BEEbo)*	*I live*
viv**es**	*(BEEbehs)*	*you live*
viv**e**	*(BEEbeh)*	*he/she/it/you (Ud). lives*
viv**imos**	*(beeBEEmos)*	*we live*
viv**ís**	*(beeBEES)*	*y'all live*
viv**en**	*(BEEbehn)*	*they/you (Uds.) live*

Vivir is an example of a 'regular' infinitive verb in Spanish. The verb expresses the action in a sentence; it tells what's happening. The basic form of the verb, its name, doesn't agree with any subject in particular. This basic form is called the "infinitive". In English, the infinitive is often identified by "to", as in "to live". In Spanish, the infinitive of a verb always ends in "r". There are three "types" of infinitives in Spanish: those that end in "–ar", such as *tomar,* those that end in "–er", like *comer,* and those, like *vivir,* that end in "–ir". To conjugate a verb, the infinitive ending must first be removed. This leaves the "stem" of the verb, to which the conjugated endings are added.

The majority of verbs of each "type" have the same set of endings when conjugated. (The regular endings for –ir verbs in the present tense are bolded in the chart above.)

So, if you know how to conjugate one regular verb of a certain type, you can conjugate any other verb of that same type. "Conjugated" forms of a verb are the forms that agree with particular subjects; as you know, there are six different conjugated forms in the present tense of Spanish verbs. English present tense verbs generally have only two different forms. For instance, "eats" is used with "he", "she" and "it", while "eat" is used with other subjects.

Verbs which share the same predictable set of conjugated endings are considered 'regular'. *Tomar, comer* and *vivir* are all regular verbs. Those verbs which do not follow the same pattern are 'irregular' (*ser* and *estar* are two irregular verbs you've learned). Knowing the correct endings for verb forms is very useful! This is especially true in Spanish, since the subject isn't always included, and so must be inferred from the verb form.

STORY

(HIYmeh ee raKEHL BEEbehn ehn OOna KAsa GRAHNdeh ahZOOL ee roSAHda)
Jaime y Raquel viven en una casa grande azul y rosada.
live in a big pink and blue house

(harDEEN pehKEHnyo kohn FLOrehs ROhas ee ahmaREEyahs)
Tienen un jardín pequeño con flores rojas y amarillas.
a small garden with red and yellow flowers

(prograhmaDOHR)
Jaime es programador. Tiene 25
a computer programmer

(Ohos BEHRdehs)
años y tiene ojos verdes.
green

(ehn hehnehRAL) (seemPAHteeko)
En general es muy simpático,

(vehs) (koLEHreeko)
pero a la vez es colérico.

(mooHEHR deh nehGOsyos)
Raquel es mujer de negocios.
a businesswoman

(kahsTAHnyos)
Tiene 26 años y tiene ojos castaños.
brown eyes

(grahSYOHsa)
Es graciosa.

(fweh ehl aMOHR ah preeMEHra BEESta)
Para los dos, fue el amor a primera vista.
for both   it was

(ehl traBAho)   *(eentehrehSAHNteh)*
El trabajo de Raquel es muy interesante.
   (Raquel's work)

(leh GOOSta MOOcho soo traBAho)
Le gusta mucho su trabajo.
(Her job pleases her a lot.)

                      (PROpyo)   *(ahbooRREEdoh)*
A Jaime no le gusta su propio trabajo. Está aburrido.
                       his own job   *He's bored.*

         (okooPAdohs)(TOHdohs los LOOnehs)
Los dos están muy ocupados. Todos los lunes,
Both of them are very busy.   *every Monday*

         (ba a sehBEEya por trehn)
Raquel va a Sevilla por tren.
   goes to Seville by train

         (MYEHRkolehs)
Todos los miércoles, Jaime va a Granada por coche.
every Wednesday

         (BYEHRnehs)   *(HOONtohs)*
Pero todos los viernes, Raquel y Jaime comen juntos en un
         every Friday   *together*

         (keh)   *(ehsTREHya ROha)*
restaurante que se llama "La Estrella Roja".
      (that's) called "The Red Star"

PRACTICE

Complete the following sentences. Use the vocabulary and the dialog to help you.

1. Jaime y Raquel viven en una _____ grande azul y rosada.

2. Jaime tiene 25 _____.

3. En general Jaime es muy _____.

4. Raquel es _____. (funny)

5. A Jaime no le gusta su _____.

6. Raquel va a Sevilla por _____.

7. Jaime va a Granada por _____.

blanco

azul

gris

marrón

negro

anaranjado

amarillo

verde

rosado

rojo

LOS COLORES

See how many colors you can remember. Fill in the crossword puzzle with the Spanish words for the colors you just learned.

DOWN

1. green
2. white
3. red
4. brown
5. yellow

ACROSS

5. orange
6. grey
7. black
8. pink

DAYS OF THE WEEK

(los DEEahs deh la sehMAHna)
los días de la semana

In English, many of the days of the week take their names from Nordic mythology. For example, "Wednesday" is "Woden's day" while "Friday" is "Friggen's day". In Spanish, on the other hand, several of the days of the week have names related to Roman mythology. *Viernes* (Friday) is *el día de Venus* while *miércoles* is *el día de Mercurio* and *martes* (Tuesday) is *el día de Marte* (Mars).

On a calendar, you'll notice that Monday, *lunes,* is considered the <u>first</u> day of the week, rather than Sunday, which is considered the <u>last</u> day of the week. *Lunes* is one exception to the Roman mythology names that most days have; it gets its name from the moon, *la luna.*

(LOOnehs)	*(MARtehs)*	*(MYEHRkolehs)*	*(HWEHvehs)*	*(BYEHRnehs)*	*(SAbadoh)*	*(dohMEENgo)*
lunes	martes	miércoles	jueves	viernes	sábado	domingo
Monday	*Tuesday*	*Wednesday*	*Thursday*	*Friday*	*Saturday*	*Sunday*

Find the days of the week hidden in the puzzle. Then circle them.

s	m	n	s	s	q	d	a	p	w	v	s	e	d	i
v	e	l	a	x	m	o	n	b	g	t	n	k	i	i
v	w	n	d	t	j	y	s	c	l	q	l	y	h	l
j	r	v	r	s	z	e	m	l	y	j	k	w	l	v
k	z	c	a	e	v	s	j	w	l	m	x	l	d	l
o	r	a	h	e	i	x	j	y	i	p	t	r	w	t
x	t	m	u	h	a	v	n	e	l	g	b	w	f	s
s	l	j	i	b	x	k	r	e	p	d	b	c	l	e
b	v	g	u	j	u	c	b	s	u	a	s	x	v	q
l	k	k	n	k	o	s	r	h	m	q	e	z	p	g
h	u	d	y	l	s	a	b	a	d	o	t	f	a	o
b	r	n	e	e	k	s	i	n	v	k	r	n	m	u
l	c	s	e	z	u	h	m	j	c	c	a	x	p	e
s	v	t	f	s	n	x	o	g	n	i	m	o	d	o
d	w	s	p	q	s	j	i	q	j	t	p	x	o	k

Put *los días de la semana* in order beginning with Monday by putting a number from 1 to 7 in front of each day.

_____ miércoles   _____ domingo   _____ martes   _____ viernes

_____ lunes   _____ sábado   _____ jueves

CHAPTER 6

(ehsTA LEHhos)
¿Está lejos?
Is it far?

Understanding directions in another language is particularly difficult, but not impossible!
Of course it helps to have *un mapa* (map) so you can look at the names of the streets as
the person you ask points to them. You don't have to understand every *palabra* (word).

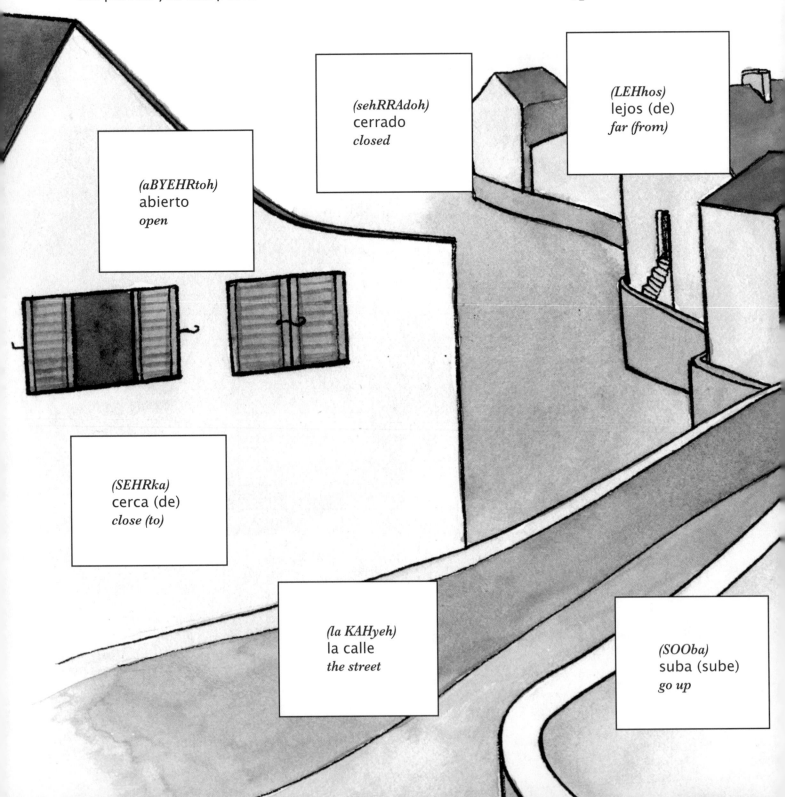

(sehRRAdoh)
cerrado
closed

(LEHhos)
lejos (de)
far (from)

(aBYEHRtoh)
abierto
open

(SEHRka)
cerca (de)
close (to)

(la KAHyeh)
la calle
the street

(SOOba)
suba (sube)
go up

VERBS USED WHEN GIVING DIRECTIONS

These verbs are in the "imperative" or "command" form for *Ud.* and for *tú*. A stranger would always use the formal *Ud.* forms when giving you directions, so these are the forms you are most likely to hear. They are listed first, followed by the informal command forms. As you can see, while English uses a "bare" infinitive (without the "to") to give commands, a specific conjugated form is used in Spanish.

camine (camina)	*(kaMEEneh)*	*walk*
tome (toma)	*(TOHmeh)*	*take*
vaya (ve)	*(BAHya) ((beh))*	*go*
vire (vira)/doble (dobla)	*(BEEreh)/ (DOHbleh)*	*turn*
suba (sube)	*(SOOba)*	*go up*
baje (baja)	*(BAHheh)*	*go down*

(kaMEEneh)
camine(camina)
walk

(BEEreh) (DOHbleh)
vire (vira)/
doble (dobla)
turn

(BAHheh)
baje (baja)
go down

(KROOseh)
cruce (cruza)
cross

al otro lado (de)
on the other side (of)

al lado de
next to, beside

(FREHNteh ah)
frente a
facing

(eesKYEHRda)
a la izquierda
to the left

(dehREHcho)
derecho/ recto
straight ahead

(dehREHcha)
a la derecha
to the right

Ir is a very common, very irregular verb. You will see forms of *ir* that appear in the dialog. You will also see the command form *ve*, as in *ve derecho*. Here is the full conjugation of *ir*:

voy	*(boy)*	*I go*
vas	*(bas)*	*you go*
va	*(ba)*	*he/she/it/you (Ud). goes*
vamos	*(BAmos)*	*we go*
vais	*(bais)*	*y'all go*
van	*(ban)*	*they/you (Uds.) go*

Ir is a very useful verb to know. One handy thing that you can do when you know how to conjugate *ir* is talk about the future. English uses "to go" in the same way, as in "I'm going to leave at three". The Spanish equivalent of the same sentence is *Voy a salir a las tres*. To make the future tense of any verb, just use the appropriate conjugated form of *ir* in the present tense, followed by *a* and the infinitive of whatever verb you want.

Vamos a visitar México en noviembre.   We're going to visit Mexico in November.

ORDINAL NUMBERS

You may need to know ordinal numbers when someone gives you directions (telling you which street to turn on). These numbers also come in handy when you need to tell which floor your hotel is on, or which floor you want to stop on in a department store.

(kyehn gaNO la kaRREHra)
¿Quién ganó la carrera?
Who won the race?

Using the numbers on the right fill in the blanks to help the race announcer list the winner and the first nine runner-ups. Say each number as you write it.

A is _____	F is _____	*(noVEHno)* noveno(9no)	*(SEHPteemo)* séptimo (7mo)
B is _____	G is _____	*(KWARtoh)* cuarto(4to)	*(okTAbo)* octavo (8vo)
C is _____	H is _____	*(preeMEHro)* primero (1ro)	*(DEHceemo)* décimo (10mo)
D is _____	I is _____	*(SEHKStoh)* sexto (6to)	*(sehGOONdoh)* segundo (2do)
E is _____	J is _____	*(KEENtoh)* quinto (5to)	*(tehrSEHro)* tercero (3ro)

DIALOG

Eduardo and Anita are standing outside a hotel, talking.
Draw the path that Anita will take on the map below.

(aDOHNdeh bas oy)
Eduardo: ¿Adónde vas hoy?
(to) where are you going today?

(boy al SEEneh)
Anita: Voy al cine.
I'm going to the cinema.

(sehRRAdoh)
Eduardo: Pero hoy es lunes. El cine está cerrado.
(eemPOHRta)
Anita: Sí, es correcto. ¡No importa! ¿Adónde vas tú?
Never mind!
(preeMEHro)   (dehsPWEHS)
Eduardo: Primero voy al banco. Después voy al
first   afterward

(PARkeh) (ehnTOHNsehs) (KOHMpras) (almaSEHN)   (KYEHrehs eer kohnMEEgo)
parque, y entonces voy de compras en un almacén.   ¿Quieres ir conmigo?
                                   department store   *Do you want to go with me?*

Anita: No, gracias. No quiero ir de compras hoy. Pienso que me gustaría visitar un
                                   I think   that I would like

museo de arte.

                (PWEHdehs) (mooSEHo deh BEHyas ARtehs) (aBYEHRtoh)
Eduardo: Puedes ir al Museo de Bellas Artes. Está abierto los lunes.
           you can go

           (ehstooPEHNdoh)   (LEHhos)
Anita: ¡Estupendo! ¿Dónde está el Museo de Bellas Artes? ¿Está lejos?

                                                        (ah pyeh)
Eduardo: No, no está muy lejos. Toma como 25 minutos a pie.
                                                        on foot

           (basTAHNteh)
Anita: ¡Ay! Está bastante lejos… Pues está bien. Es buen día para dar un paseo.
           Wow! That's pretty far…   *well*   *It's a good day to take a walk.*

                (a behr) (beh dehREHcho)   (KAHyeh) (eesKYEHRda)
Eduardo: Tienes razón. A ver… ve derecho y toma la primera calle a la izquierda. Es la
                let's see…

           (SEEgeh)   (AHSta yehGAR) (ahvehNEEda koLOHN)
Calle Bolívar. Sigue la Calle Bolívar hasta llegar a la Avenida Colón. Entonces dobla a la derecha.
           follow/continue   *until you get to*

Anita: A la izquierda en la Calle Bolívar, a la derecha en la Avenida Colón.

                                                        (KROOsa ehl PWEHNteh)
Eduardo: Sigue derecho en la Avenida Colón hasta llegar al puente. Cruza el puente y

                (eenmehdDYAtaMEHNteh)
dobla a la izquierda inmediatamente.

                            (krooSAR)
Anita: Bueno, doblo a la izquierda después de cruzar el puente.

Eduardo: Correcto. Vas a ver el museo a la derecha.
                you'll see

Anita: Gracias, Eduardo. ¡Hasta luego!

                (deesFROOta)
Eduardo: ¡Hasta luego! Disfruta el paseo.
                enjoy

CHAPTER 7

(keh ehstaSYOHN prehFYEHrehs)
¿Qué estación prefieres?
Which season do you prefer?

(ehn Otras paLAbras)
en otras palabras
in other words

(a mee tahmBYEHN)
¡Yo también!/¡A mí también!
Me too!

(ehn mee opeeNYON)
en mi opinión
in my opinion

THE SEASONS OF THE YEAR

(las estaSYOnehs dehl Anyo)
las estaciones del año

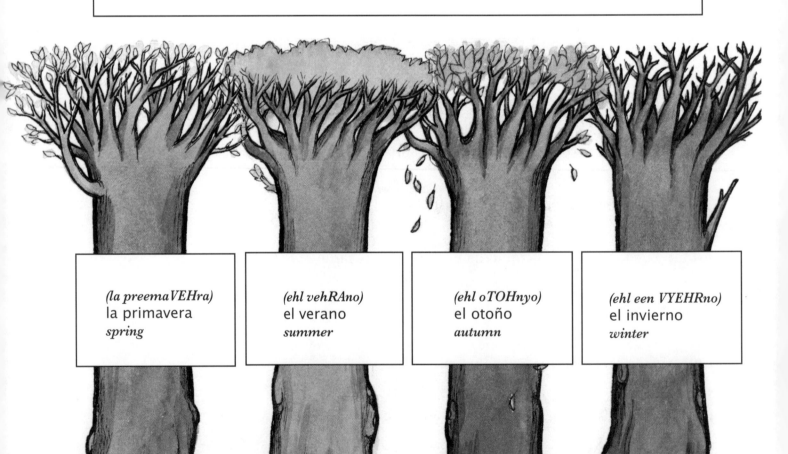

(la preemaVEHra)
la primavera
spring

(ehl vehRAno)
el verano
summer

(ehl oTOHnyo)
el otoño
autumn

(ehl een VYEHRno)
el invierno
winter

THE MONTHS OF THE YEAR

(MEHsehs)
los meses del año

Unlike the seasons, all the months have Spanish names that are similar to their English names. In Spanish, the names of months and days of the week are not capitalized.

(ehNEHro)
enero

(fehBREHro)
febrero

(MARso)
marzo

(aBREEL)
abril

(MAHyo)
mayo

(HOOnyo)
junio

(HOOlyo)
julio

(aGOHStoh)
agosto

(sehTYEHMbreh)
septiembre

(ohkTOObreh)
octubre

(noBYEHMbreh)
noviembre

(deeSYEHMbreh)
diciembre

STORY

Look at the pictures and read the sentences under each one. See if you can figure out *el significado* (meaning). Write what you think the sentences mean in the blanks. Use the vocabulary and idioms to help you *comprender* (understand) the story that follows the pictures.

(la MAdreh)	*(el PAdreh)*	*(ehl ehrMAno)*	*(la ehrMAna)*	*(la faMEElya)*
la madre	el padre	el hermano	la hermana	la familia
mother	*father*	*brother*	*sister*	*family*

La madre está en la playa en el verano.

1. _____

El padre está en las montañas en el invierno.

2. _____

El hermano da un paseo por el desierto en el otoño.

3. _____

Las hermanas recogen las flores en la primavera.

4. _____

(peeLAR gooTYEHrres)

Me llamo Pilar Gutiérrez. Tengo veinte años. Tengo una familia muy interesante. Somos

(seeEHMpreh)

todos muy diferentes. Cuando tomamos vacaciones, mi madre siempre quiere ir a la
all   *always*

(mohnTAnyas)

playa, pero a mi padre le gustan las montañas. En otras palabras, a mi madre le gusta

(prehFYEHreh)

tomar vacaciones en el verano, particularmente en agosto. Mi padre prefiere el invierno.
prefers

(ehskeeAR)

Le gusta esquiar en diciembre o enero. A mi hermano, Arturo, que tiene 17, le gusta
to ski

(por ehl BOSkeh)

dar un paseo por el bosque. Le gustan los colores de otoño (anaranjado, rojo, amarillo,
through the woods

(ehrmaNEEta)

marrón). Por eso prefiere tomar vacaciones en septiembre u octubre. A mi hermanita,
so   *little sister*

Mercedes, que tiene 15, le gusta la primavera. ¡A mi también! A Mercedes y a mí nos
to us

(BEHyas)   *(seen ehmBARgo)*

encantan todas las flores bellas en la primavera. Sin embargo, a mi hermana no le gusta
are delightful   *beautiful*   *however*

(byaHAR)   *(mehHOrehs)*

viajar. En mi opinión, marzo, abril y mayo son los meses mejores para viajar.
to travel   *best*

¿Cuándo tomamos vacaciones? ¡Por todo el año! Damos un paseo por el bosque todos
All year long!

los sábados en septiembre. De vez en cuando damos un paseo por el bosque también en
from time to time

(FEEnehs)

el invierno y la primavera. Por supuesto esquiamos muchos fines de semana en diciembre,
weekends

(a mehNOOdoh BAmos)

enero y febrero. En junio, julio y agosto a menudo vamos a la playa. También
often   *we go*

(kehDAmos)

nos quedamos en casa mucho. Todos están contentos.
we stay home a lot   *everyone*

PRACTICE

. Now try to translate these sentences into *español*.

1. I'm 20 years old. _____.

2. He likes the colors of autumn (orange, red, yellow, brown).

   _____.

3. Me too! Mercedes and I love the beautiful flowers.

   _____.

4. In June, July, and August we often go to the beach.

   _____.

(NOUN) GENDER

All Spanish nouns are either masculine or feminine in "gender." Sometimes it's easy to figure out which group a noun belongs to as in *un americano,* an American man, and *una americana,* an American woman. Other times it just doesn't seem to make sense: *una corbata* (a necktie) is feminine and *el maquillaje* (make-up) is masculine. The gender of nouns is really a grammatical property rather than an expression of biological gender.

Try to learn the noun markers *(el, la, un, or una)* together with the nouns: *la playa, la flor, la primavera, el mes, una familia, un día.* This will help you a lot in remembering the gender. Sometimes you can tell the gender of a word by its ending, though not always.

These endings tend to be feminine:
-a   la playa
-ción   la nación
-sión   la televisión
-dad   la ciudad (the city)

*A common exception is *el mapa,* the map.

These endings tend to be masculine:
-o   el libro (the book)
-ema   el sistema
-ama   el programa

*A common exception is *la mano,* the hand.

Other endings vary as to whether they occur on masculine or feminine words, so it's always a good idea to learn the gender as part of the word.

Words that "go with" nouns, like articles and adjectives, also may have different forms, depending on the gender of the noun they go with. For example, let's consider the articles. The articles of English are "the" and "a(n)". In Spanish, as you might expect, there are 4 different ways of saying "the" (the definite article): *el, la, los, las.*

FEMININE

la madre *(feminine singular)*

las hermanas *(feminine plural)*

MASCULINE

el padre *(masculine singular)*

los hermanos *(masculine plural)*

PRACTICE

Choose the definite article that goes with each noun.
You may have to look back at previous chapters!

1. _____ hermana

2. _____ playa

3. _____ familia

4. _____ queso

5. _____ coche

6. _____ hombre

7. _____ mañana

8. _____ estación

9. _____ museo

10. _____ calle

There are also 4 different ways of saying "a" (the indefinite article). Unlike English, Spanish has plural forms of the indefinite article (the closest thing in English would be "some"):

una casa *(feminine singular)*

unas montañas *(feminine plural)*

un mes *(masculine singular)*

unos parques *(masculine plural)*

CHAPTER 8

(EHSta ehs mee faMEElya)
Ésta es mi familia.
This is my family.

There is a good chance that if you make *un amigo hispano / una amiga hispana,* you will be introduced to some of his or her family members at some point. Not only is it important to be able to understand these words that show family relationships, but it's also useful to be able to introduce and talk about the members of your *familia.*

(ehl sohm-BREHro)
el sombrero
hat

(KORtoh)
corto
short

(ALtoh)
alto
tall

(ehl PEHlo)
el pelo
hair

(LARgo)
largo
long

(BAho)
bajo
short

(ehl ehsPOso)
el esposo
husband

(la ehsPOsa)
la esposa
wife

LA FAMILIA

MALE

el padre	*(PAdreh)*	*father*
el abuelo	*(aBWEHlo)*	*grandfather*
el suegro	*(SWEHgro)*	*father-in-law*
el hermano	*(ehrMAno)*	*brother*
el hijo	*(EEho)*	*son*
el nieto	*(NYEHtoh)*	*grandson*
el tío	*(TEEoh)*	*uncle*
el sobrino	*(soBREEno)*	*nephew*
el esposo	*(ehsPOso)*	*husband*
los padres	*(PAdrehs)*	*parents*

FEMALE

la madre	*(MAdreh)*	*mother*
la abuela	*(aBWEHla)*	*grandmother*
la suegra	*(SWEHgra)*	*mother-in-law*
la hermana	*(ehrMAna)*	*sister*
la hija	*(EEha)*	*daughter*
la nieta	*(NYEHta)*	*granddaughter*
la tía	*(TEEa)*	*aunt*
la sobrina	*(soBREEna)*	*niece*
la esposa	*(ehsPOsa)*	*wife*
los padres	*(PAdrehs)*	*parents*

STORY

(PEHdro)   (kaNOso)
Pedro tiene una familia pequeña. Su madre se llama Sofía. Tiene pelo corto canoso y es
                                                                                                    gray-haired

(deeNAmeeka)   (roDOHLfo)   (yehBAR)
muy dinámica. Su padre se llama Rodolfo. Es alto y le gusta llevar sombreros.   Pedro
                                                                                    wear

(paTREEsyo)
no tiene hermana, pero tiene un hermano, Patricio, a quien ama mucho. Patricio es muy
                                        whom he loves a lot

(kaSAdoh)   (maREEna)
gracioso y está casado con Marina, la cuñada de Pedro. Ella tiene pelo largo negro y es
        is married to

                                                                                (aMAlya)
bella y muy simpática. No tienen hijos. La esposa de Pedro se llama Amalia. Ella es

                                                                                (ehLEHna)
baja, tiene pelo castaño, y es muy inteligente. La suegra de Pedro es Elena y su esposo es

(alBEHRtoh)
Alberto, el suegro de Pedro.

Pedro y Amalia tienen una hija que se llama Natalia. Ella tiene 11 años y

                                                                (naTAlya)   (ehNEHRheeka)
ama mucho a su familia, particularmente a sus abuelos. Natalia es muy enérgica. De

        (koRREHR) (hooGAR) (dehPORteh)   (GWApo)
hecho, necesita correr o jugar un deporte todos los días. ¿Y Pedro? Es guapo, pero no
            to run   *to play*   *a sport*   *everyday*   *handsome*

muy inteligente.

PRACTICE

Fill in the blanks under each picture.
  a) Write the name of the person.
  b) Write what relationship that person is to Pedro. (Be sure to include the definite article *el, la, los, las* before the word.)

1. a _____
   b _____
2. a _____
   b _____

3. a _____
   b _____
4. a _____
   b _____

(Pedro)

5. a _____
   b _____

6. a _____
   b _____
7. a _____
   b _____

8. a _____
   b _____

A. Read the passage again. Are the following statements *ciertas* (C) or *falsas* (F)?

1. Pedro es el tío de Natalia. _____

2. Patricio y Elena son esposo y esposa. _____

3. Amalia es la madre de Natalia. _____

4. Natalia es la nieta de Rodolfo. _____

5. Pedro y Patricio son hermanos. _____

6. Natalia es la sobrina de Patricio. _____

7. Sofía es la suegra de Pedro. _____

B. Now see if you can answer these questions. Check your answers in the back of the book.

1. ¿Quién es muy inteligente? _____
   who

2. ¿Quién tiene pelo corto canoso? _____

3. ¿Quién está casado con Marina? _____

4. ¿Quién ama a sus abuelos? _____

5. ¿Quién es guapo? _____

ADJECTIVES

In Chapter 7, you learned about grammatical "gender" in Spanish. Adjectives, which describe nouns, agree with them in gender and in number. Many types of adjectives, though not all, have a different ending in the feminine. Here are some examples:

M		F	
-o	/	-a	bajo/baja
-or	/	-ora	trabajador/trabajadora (hard-working)
-ol	/	-ola	español/española
-on	/	-ona	cabezón/cabezona (stubborn)
-e	/	-e	inteligente/inteligente

To make an adjective plural, add *–s* if the singular form ends in a vowel *(española/españolas)* and *–es* if the singular form ends in a consonant *(español/españoles)*.

Unlike in English, in Spanish most adjectives occur after the noun. An important exception to this rule is adjectives indicating quantity, such as numbers, or *mucho, poco,* etc. This type of adjective occurs before the noun it modifies.

una mujer bella   unos libros interesantes   muchas personas altas

In the following exercise, add the adjectives (in parentheses) to the following nouns. Be sure to use the correct form of the adjective (masculine or feminine, singular or plural), and put the adjective in the correct place in relation to the noun. The first one is done for you.

1. La mujer (alto)   la mujer alta _____

2. La hija (bajo)   _____

3. Los hombres (español)   _____

4. La abuela (trabajador)   _____

5. La sobrina (inteligente) _____

6. Los padres (inteligente) _____

POSSESSIVE ADJECTIVES

Words like "my, your, his, her" are possessive adjectives. Look at the chart below. Notice that in contrast to English, the possessive adjectives in Spanish agree with the thing possessed in gender and number.

WITH FEMININE NOUNS		WITH MASCULINE NOUNS
(mee) mi tía mis tías	MY	mi tío mis tíos
(too) tu tía tus tías	YOUR (tú)	tu tío tus tíos
(soo) su tía sus tías	YOUR (Ud., Uds.)	su tío sus tíos
su tía sus tías	HIS/HER	su tío sus tíos
(NWEHStra) nuestra tía nuestras tías	OUR	*(NWEHStro)* nuestro tío nuestros tíos
(BWEHStra) vuestra tía vuestras tías	YOUR (vosotros)	*(BWEHStro)* vuestro tío vuestros tíos
su tía sus tías	THEIR	su tío sus tíos

CHAPTER 9

(AHseh dehmaSYAdoh FREEo)
¡Hace demasiado frío!
It's too cold!

Being able to chat about *el tiempo* (the weather) is a useful skill to have in another language. Whether you're at a bus stop, *en un restaurante,* or making small talk with a desk clerk at a hotel, *el tiempo* is a safe, popular topic (and often necessary if you're planning outdoor activities).

¿Qué tiempo hace?
What's the weather like?

(aRREEba los koraZOnehs)
¡Arriba los corazones!
Keep your chin up!

(kehREEdoh/ kehREEda)
querido/a
dear

WEATHER EXPRESSIONS

(OOmehdoh)
Está húmedo.
It's humid.

(FREEo)
Hace frío.
It's cold.

(BYEHNtoh)
Hace viento.
It's windy.

(yoBYEHNdoh)
Está lloviendo.
It's raining.

(sohl)
Hace sol.
It's sunny.

Hace (muy) buen tiempo.
It's a beautiful day.

Hace muy mal tiempo.
The weather is horrible.

(nehBAHNdoh)
Está nevando.
It's snowing.

This is a telephone conversation between *Elisa y su madre. Elisa tiene 22 años* and is living in Alaska for 1 year doing research as part of her university graduate studies. *Su madre vive en Quito.*

          (maMA)
Elisa: Buenas tardes, Mamá.
           Mom

Mamá: Hola, querida. ¿Cómo estás?

Elisa: Estoy bien excepto que tengo frío.

Mamá: Pobrecita. ¿Está nevando?

Elisa: Mamá, es invierno y estoy en Alaska.

        (monTOHN)
¡Por supuesto! Nieva un montón aquí.
          a ton

¿Qué tiempo hace en Quito?

              (EEso)
Mamá: Está lloriendo mucho hoy, pero ayer hizo sol.
               it was sunny

De hecho, hizo bastante calor ayer, pero hace

fresco hoy. Mañana va a hacer sol de nuevo.
 cool   *It's going to be sunny again.*

    (BWEHLbehs)
¿Cuándo vuelves a casa?
When are you coming home?
            (okooPAda)
Elisa: No sé. Estoy muy ocupada con mis
    I don't know.   *busy*

investigaciones. Trabajo todos los días
    research

excepto los domingos.

Mamá: *(dyos MEEo)* ¡Dios mío! ¿Dónde trabajas?
My goodness!

Elisa: *(BWEHlo)* Vuelo a Nome todos los lunes y me quedo *(meh KEHdoh)* dos días.
I fly   *I stay*

A menudo voy a Fairbanks también, por coche.

¡Está lejos de aquí! Prefiero trabajar en Anchorage.

(Otra behs) Tengo que ir otra vez a Fairbanks el viernes.
again

(BYEHnehs) ¿Cuándo vienes a visitarme?
When are you coming to visit me?

Mamá: *(aOra)* ¡Dios mío, no ahora! ¡No en el invierno! *(SAbehs)* Sabes que no me gusta la nieve. *(NYEHbeh)*
not now   *you know that*   *the snow*

Quiero ir a Alaska en el verano cuando hace calor.

Elisa: Bien. Sí, hace demasiado frío aquí en el invierno.

Tal vez vuelvo a casa para las vacaciones.
maybe

Mamá: *(eeDEHa magNEEfeeka)* ¡Qué idea magnífica! Ven a casa, querida. Como
                                    come home   *as*
sabes, hace sol aquí de vez en cuando. ¡Y no hay nieve! *(ay)*
you know   *from time to time*   *And there's no snow!*

Elisa: Bueno, Mamá. Nos vemos pronto.
                                      soon

Mamá: Hasta luego, querida.

¡Arriba los corazones!

¿COMPRENDES?

Do you understand?

See if you can answer the following questions based on the dialog.

¿Quién tiene frío? _____

¿Dónde está Elisa? _____

¿Dónde está lloviendo? _____

¿Cuándo trabaja Elisa? _____

¿Cuándo quiere su madre visitar Alaska? _____

See if you can match each statement on the right to the appropriate picture of the person to make each statement true. Connect each of the circles with a line.

(1) Dice que está lloviendo.
says

(2) Tiene frío.

(3) Trabaja del lunes al sábado.

(4) No le gusta la nieve.

(5) Va al trabajo por avión y por coche.

(6) Quiere ir a Alaska en el verano.

(7) Va a volver a casa en diciembre.

(8) Le gusta trabajar en Anchorage.

PRACTICE

Now try to complete the sentences with the weather expressions given. (You can peek back at Chapter 7 to review *los meses y las estaciones*.)

1. En el verano _____.
   it is hot

2. En abril _____.
   it rains a lot

3. En noviembre _____.
   the weather is horrible

4. En enero _____.
   it snows

5. En la primavera _____.
   it is windy

6. En julio _____.
   it's humid

7. Hoy _____.
   it's a beautiful day

Here are more handy expressions you can use to talk about the past and the future:

	(anteh-aYEHR)
la semana pasada	anteayer
last week	*the day before yesterday*
la semana que viene	pasado mañana
next week	*the day after tomorrow*

You may recall the words *ayer (yesterday)* and *hoy (today)* from Chapter 6 when you learned about giving directions. Now let's add *mañana (tomorrow)* to your vocabulary. (Remember how *Mamá* described the weather in *Quito?*)

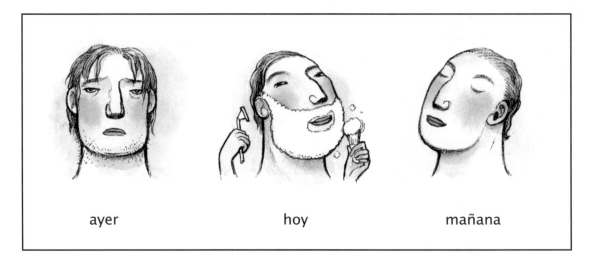

ayer   hoy   mañana

PRACTICE AND REVIEW

See if you can figure out which word doesn't belong in each of the series of words below. Write the words in the blanks.

_____ 1. calor, verano, sol, nieve

_____ 2. ayer, frío, mañana, hoy

_____ 3. mucho, cuándo, dónde, quién

_____ 4. trabaja, visita, aquí, va

_____ 5. día, semana, año, primavera

VERB CONJUGATION

HACER
to make/to do

hago	*(AHgo)*	*I make/do*
haces	*(AHsehs)*	*you make/do*
hace	*(AHseh)*	*he/she/it/you (Ud). makes/does*
hacemos	*(ahSEHmos)*	*we make/do*
hacéis	*(ahSEHYS)*	*y'all make/do*
hacen	*(AHsehn)*	*they/you (Uds.) make/do*

Here are some useful expresions with *"hacer"*:

hace poco
a short time ago

La vi hace poco.
I saw her a short time ago.

(aehroPWEHRtoh)

hacer cola
to stand in line

Tenemos que hacer cola en el aeropuerto.
We have to stand in line at the airport.

hacer la maleta
to pack (a suitcase)

¿Haces la maleta para el viaje?
Are you packing for the trip?

hacer un viaje
to take a trip

Quiero hacer un viaje a España.
I want to take a trip to Spain.

hacer una pregunta
to ask a question

Rafael hace muchas preguntas en clase.
Rafael asks lots of questions in class.

CHAPTER 10

¿Tienes la hora, por favor?
Do you have the time, please?

You've learned *los días de la semana* (Chapter 5) *y los meses del año* (Chapter 7). Now you'll learn about how to tell time. If you need to, go back to Chapters 2 and 4 to review *los números* up to 22. Later in this chapter you'll learn some more numbers that you can use in order to say the minutes.

(ooMOR)
estar de buen humor
to be in a good mood

estar de mal humor
to be in a bad mood

(tehmPRAno)
llegar temprano
to arrive early

(TARdeh)
llegar tarde
to arrive late

(ehstaSYON)
estación de tren
train station

(beeYEHteh)
billete
ticket

(anDEHN)
andén
track/platform

(MEESmo/a)
mismo/a
same

(meeNOOtoh)
minuto
minute

(asohmBROso)
asombroso
amazing

DIALOG

(BYAHhan)
Antonio y Frida llegan a la estación de tren. Viajan por tren a León para visitar a unos amigos.
they are traveling by train

(pooDYEHra dehSEER)
Antonio: Por favor, ¿me pudiera decir cuándo sale el próximo tren para León?
could you tell/say   leaves

Empleado: Sale a las 10:19.

Antonio: ¿Cómo? ¿A qué hora?

Empleado: A las 10:19, Señor.

Antonio: ¿Y qué hora es?

Empleado: Son las 10:16. Uds. tienen 3 minutos.

Antonio le dice a Frida: ¡Hay un tren en 3 minutos!

Frida: ¡Caramba! Llegamos demasiado tarde.
too

Antonio: Siempre es la misma historia.

Siempre llegamos tarde.

Frida: Estás de mal humor

esta mañana, ¿no?

Antonio: ¡Basta!

That's enough!

59

Frida *(al empleado)*: ¿A qué hora sale el próximo tren para León?

No podemos tomar este tren.

Empleado: A ver... el próximo tren para León sale a las 13:47.

Frida mira a Antonio.

Antonio: Chévere.
That's cool.

Frida *(al empleado)* : Está bien. Dos billetes, por favor.

Empleado: De ida o de ida y vuelta?
one way or roundtrip.

Frida: De ida y vuelta, por favor. De segunda clase.

Empleado: Son 30 Euros. Aquí están sus billetes.

Frida: Gracias. ¿Cuál andén?

Empleado: El andén número ocho.

¡Buen viaje!
Have a good trip!

Antonio *(a Frida)*: Bueno, pues...

¿quieres tomar algo?
Do you want to have something to drink?

Frida: ¡Con mucho gusto! Es asombroso.

¡Estás de buen humor ahora!

Antonio: Por supuesto. Porque ahora no llegamos tarde.

¡Llegamos temprano! ¡Vamos!

Answer *cierto* or *falso* to the following statements based on the dialog.

1. Antonio y Frida viajan por avión.
   plane
   _____

2. Antonio pregunta qué hora es.
   asks
   _____

3. Antonio piensa que Frida está de mal humor.
   thinks that
   _____

4. Frida pide tres billetes.
   asks for
   _____

5. Hacen un viaje de ida y vuelta.
   _____

TELLING TIME

¿Qué hora es?

Expressing time in *español* is easy. Just remember to use the verb *ser* and a feminine definite article (feminine to agree with *hora*). Both the verb and the article will be singular if it's the one o'clock hour, and plural any other time. For example, you would say *Es la una y cinco* but *Son las dos y cinco.*

In *países hispanohablantes,* the 24-hour system of telling time ("military" time, as we call it in the U.S.) is usually used to avoid ambiguity on TV and radio, as well as with travel schedules, appointments, and theater and concert times. Just subtract 12 to figure out the time you are familiar with in the U.S. (16 hours is 16–12= 4 PM) It's usually a good idea to say *de la mañana, de la noche,* etc. when using the 12-hour clock, unless it's clear from the context that it's a.m. or p.m.

Son las siete   Es mediodía.   Son las tres   Son las ocho
de la mañana.   de la tarde.   de la noche.

                     (mehdyoDEEa)
por la mañana   el mediodía   por la tarde   por la noche
in the morning   *noon*   *in the afternoon* *in the evening*

It's easy to add the minutes when you are telling time:

Son las once y cuarenta
de la noche.

Son las siete y
veinte de la mañana.

Son las dos menos
diez de la tarde.

Son las nueve y
media de la mañana.

To say "a quarter after" the hour, you can use *y cuarto*. If it's a quarter 'til, you can say *"menos cuarto"*. (*Menos* is used to express a number of minutes before the hour.) To tell the half-hour, use *y media*.

PRACTICE

¿Qué hora es?

Match the times with the clocks. Write the correct letter under each clock.

a. Son las diez y cuarto. b. Son las cuatro menos quince. c. Son las once y treinta y ocho.

d. Son las cinco y media.   e. Son las ocho y cuarenta y siete.

1. _____   2. _____   3. _____   4. _____   5. _____

LOS NÚMEROS 23-100

You'll need to know higher *números* if you want to *comprender los minutos* when someone tells you the time (...not to mention how important these numbers are for shopping or even revealing your age if the situation presents itself). Read the pronunciation carefully and say each number out loud.

23	veintitrés	*(vehyntee TREHS)*	40	cuarenta	*(kwaREHNta)*
24	veinticuatro	*(vehynteeKWAtro)*	50	cincuenta	*(seenKWEHNta)*
25	veinticinco		60	sesenta	*(sehSEHNta)*
26	veintiséis		70	setenta	*(sehTEHNta)*
27	veintisiete		71	setenta y uno	
28	veintiocho		72	setenta y dos	
29	veintinueve		80	ochenta	*(oCHEHNta)*
30	treinta	*(TREHYNta)*	90	noventa	*(noBEHNta)*
31	treinta y uno		95	noventa y cinco	
32	treinta y dos		100	cien	*(syehn)*

DECIR
(to say/tell)

digo	*(DEEgo)*	*I say/tell*
dices	*(DEEsehs)*	*you say/tell*
dice	*(DEEseh)*	*he/she/it/you (Ud.) says/tells*
decimos	*(dehSEEmos)*	*we say/tell*
decís	*(dehSEES)*	*y'all say/tell*
dicen	*(DEEsehn)*	*they/you (Uds.) say/tell*

CHAPTER 11

(LEEbreh)
¿Qué haces en tu tiempo libre?
What do you do in your free time?

(poolKREEseemo)
pulcrísimo/a
neat as a pin

(GAyos)
con el canto de los gallos
at the crack of dawn

(koseeNEHro ehpeeKOOreo)
un cocinero epicúreo
a real gourmet cook

FOCUS: PREPOSITIONS

en
in

(ehnFREHNteh)
enfrente de
in front of

(deBAho)
debajo de
under

(DEHNtro)
dentro de
inside

(SObreh)
en/sobre
on

(dehTRAS)
detrás de
behind

(FWEHra)
fuera de
outside (of)

al lado de
next to

USEFUL EXPRESSIONS

(ay)
hay
there is/there are

(nabehGAR la rrehth)
navegar la red
surf the Web

(mahnDAR koRREHo ehlehkTROneeko)
mandar correo electrónico
send email

VOCABULARY

(aRREEba)
arriba
upstairs

(aBAho)
abajo
downstairs

(PEHrro)
el perro
dog

(pehrSOHNas)
las personas
people

(BYEHho)
viejo/a
old

el gato
cat

(kompootaDOHra)
la computadora
computer

(HObehn)
joven
young

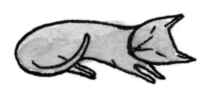

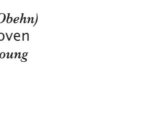

65

STORY

Sami es un perro marrón pequeño.

Vive en una casa con una gata negra que se llama Mala.

También hay tres personas que viven en la casa: una mujer, un hombre viejo

y un chico joven. Su casa es muy bella y pulcrísima.

(mehNOOdoh)
Sami visita a menudo a Tonio, el chico de 7 años,
      often

en su cuarto arriba. A Sami le gusta
   room

      (MYEHNtras) *(TOHnyo)(HWEHga)*
sentarse en la cama mientras que Tonio juega con
to sit   *the bed*   *while*   *plays with*

(hooGEHtehs)   *(DWEHRmeh)*
sus juguetes. Mala, la gata, duerme debajo de la cama.
his toys   *sleeps*

     (tohMAS)   *(okooPARseh)*
El abuelo de Tonio, Tomás, le gusta ocuparse en la

(koSEEna)   *(koseeNAR)*
cocina. ¡Le encanta cocinar!
the kitchen   He loves to cook!

De hecho, es un cocinero epicúreo. A Sami le gusta sentarse al lado del horno y oler la
                           the oven   to smell

comida deliciosa. Mala duerme en la alfombra enfrente de la ventana.
             the rug   *the window*

(konSWEHlo)
A Sami le gusta dormir hasta tarde, pero Consuelo,
to sleep late

la madre de Tonio, se levanta con el
gets up

(ehnSYEHNdeh)
canto de los gallos, baja a la oficina y enciende
turns on

la computadora. Lee su correo
she reads

(naBEHga)   *(basooREHro)*
electrónico y navega la red. Mala duerme dentro del basurero. A Consuelo también le

gusta leer novelas y trabajar en el jardín en su tiempo libre.
to read

A Tonio le gusta tocar el piano.
to play

(soFA)
Sami se esconde detrás del sofá en la
hides

sala cuando Tonio toca el piano.

(RUYdoh)
A Mala no le gusta el ruido así que va
the noise so

afuera y duerme en el jardín.
outdoors

Casi todos los viernes, Tomás, Consuelo y Tonio van arriba para mirar la tele,
almost   *to watch TV*

(NAYpehs)
leer o jugar a los naipes en la sala de juegos. Mala duerme en la silla suave y Sami se
play   *cards*   *the game room*   *the soft chair*

(Komoda)
relaja en el piso cerca de su familia. Sami tiene una vida bastante cómoda.
relaxes   *the floor*   *a very comfortable life*

DO YOU UNDERSTAND?

Match the members of the family with the things they like to do.
Write the letters in the blanks.

1. Sami _____   A. tocar el piano

2. Mala _____   B. cocinar

3. Consuelo _____   C. dormir

4. Tomás _____   D. sentarse en la cama

5. Tonio _____   E. navegar la red

Here is a <u>regular</u> –ar verb that functions in a special way:

	(goosTAR)	
	GUSTAR	
	to please	
gusto	*(GOOStoh)*	*I please*
gustas	*(GOOStas)*	*you please*
gusta	*(GOOSta)*	*he/she/it/you (Ud). pleases*
gustamos	*(goosTAHmos)*	*we please*
gustáis	*(goosTAHYS)*	*y'all please*
gustan	*(GOOStahn)*	*they/you (Uds.) please*

Since *gustar* means "to please" or "to be pleasing" rather than "to like", it is used with an object pronoun that tells who is being pleased. *Gustar* is most often used in the third-person forms, to agree with the thing or things that are pleasing to someone. Here are some examples of how *gustar* is used:

Me gusta el café.
Coffee pleases me/ I like coffee.

¿Te gustan los buñuelos?
Are fritters pleasing to you/ Do you like fritters?

68

Just like *gustar* is a mirror image of the verb "to please", *encantar* might be considered the mirror image of "to love", especially when used to talk about one's affinity for things or activities. When referring to people, "to love" can be directly translated using *querer* (see Chapter 4) or *amar,* which is a regular –ar verb. The usage of these two verbs varies, but *querer* is more common in general.

Gramatically, *encantar* functions the same way as *gustar*. Whatever is doing the pleasing or enchanting is the subject, and the individual being pleased is expressed as an indirect object of the verb. Thus, the verb *encantar,* like *gustar,* is always used with an indirect object pronoun.

Use the picture below to help you fill in the blanks with:

debajo de, dentro de, al lado de sobre o detrás de.

1. El abuelo está _____ la cama.
2. Hay un gato _____ la cama.
3. La cama está _____ la alfombra.
4. La ventana está _____ la cama.
5. Hay juguetes _____ la cama.
6. Hay un basurero _____ la cama.

Now write 2 sentences of your own describing the picture.

1. _____.

2. _____.

CHAPTER 12

(paSASteh oon bwehn feen deh sehMAna)
¿Pasaste un buen fin de semana?
Did you have a good weekend?

Vicente: Buenos días, Mónica. ¿Pasaste un buen fin de semana?

Mónica: Hola, Vicente¡ Sí! Fue excelente
it was

(eeSEESteh)
Vicente: ¿De veras? ¿Qué hiciste?
Really? What did you do?

(hooGEH)   *(fwee)*
Mónica: Jugué tenis con mi hermana el sábado. El domingo por la noche fui a un
I played   *I went*

concierto –¡los Rolling Stones! ¡Fue estupendo!

                    (MOOseeka)(frankaMEHNteh)
Vicente: Me encanta su música. Francamente,
      I love their music.   *frankly*

(sorPREHNdeh) (tohdaBEEa)
me soprende que todavía den conciertos.
                still   they give

Mónica: Sí, son viejos, pero a pesar de
                    in spite of that
      (CHEHbehrehs)
eso son bien chéveres.
      really cool

¿Qué hiciste tú este fin de semana?

(hooGASteh)   *(SYEHMpreh)*
¿Jugaste al fútbol como siempre?
did you play

Vicente: Jugué fútbol el sábado y ayer jugué
un poco de básquetbol. Anoche vi una película
con mi sobrino.   *I saw*

           (BYEHron)
Mónica: ¿Qué película vieron?
           did you see
   (BEEmos)
Vicente: Vimos la nueva de Harry Potter.
   we saw the new one

Mónica: ¿Y fue buena?

(dyoh)

Vicente: Sí. A mi sobrino, que tiene 8 años, le dio un poco de miedo,
it scared him a little

(pehnSEH)   *(deebehrTEEda)*
pero yo pensé que fue muy divertida.
I thought   *fun/entertainig*

Mónica: Mi hermana quiere verla, pero yo prefiero
wants to see it

las películas románticas.

Vicente: ¿De veras? Yo también las prefiero.
them

Mónica: ¡No me digas! Me estás bromeando.
No way!

(prehGOONtaleh)
Vicente: No, ¡es la verdad! Pregúntale a Julia.
it's true!   *Ask Julia.*

Sabe que me gustan las películas románticas.
she knows

Bueno, ¡adiós! Me voy. ¡Tengo que trabajar!

Mónica: ¿Julia? ¡Espera! ¿Qué hay entre tú y Julia? ¡Estoy harta con tus secretos!
Wait!   *between*

(reooNYOHN)
Vicente: ¡Nos vemos en la reunión a las diez!
meeting

Mónica *(gritando)* : ¡Caramba! ¿Qué reunión?

MATCHING

Match the questions and statements on the left with the appropriate responses on the right.

_____ 1. ¿Y fue buena?

_____ 2. Vi una película anoche.

_____ 3. Me estás bromeando.

_____ 4. ¿Pasaste un buen fin de semana?

_____ 5. ¿Cómo fue el concierto?
　　　　　　how

_____ 6. ¿Qué hiciste tú este fin de semana?

a) Sí, fue excelente.

b) Jugué fútbol.

c) ¡Fue estupendo!

d) No, ¡es la verdad!

e) ¿Qué película vieron?

f) Sí.

FOCUS

SIMPLE PAST TENSE (PRETÉRITO)

There are several past tenses in Spanish, as there are in English. The simple past tense or "preterit" is very commonly used in both Spanish and English. This is the tense used to talk about what <u>happened</u> in the past (rather than what <u>was happening</u> or what <u>has happened</u>, for example).

These following sentences have their verbs conjugated in the *pretérito*:

<u>Salí</u> del cuarto.   *I left the room.*
Él me <u>dio</u> un regalo.   *He gave me a present.*
<u>Vivieron</u> en Uruguay por un año.   *They lived in Uruguay for a year.*
La fiesta <u>fue</u> ayer.   *The party was yesterday.*
¿<u>Fuiste</u> a la tienda hoy?   *Did you go to the store today?*
<u>Vimos</u> una película anoche.   *We saw a movie last night.*

Pensar is an example of an –ar verb which is regular in the *pretérito*. Remember, before adding the conjugated endings, you'll want to remove the "–ar" from the infinitive.

	(pehnSAR)	
	P E N S A R	
	to think	
pensé	*(pehnSEH)*	*I thought*
pensaste	*(pehnSASteh)*	*you thought*
pensó	*(pehnSO)*	*he/she/it/you (Ud). thought*
pensamos	*(pehnSAmos)*	*we thought*
pensasteis	*(pehnSASteys)*	*y'all thought*
pensaron	*(pehnSAron)*	*they/you (Uds.) thought*

Now that you know how to conjugate any regular verb in the preterit, let's look at three important verbs that are irregular in the preterit. First, take a look at the preterit forms of *ir* and *ser;* their forms are identical! Once again, context should help you figure out which is which. For instance, consider these two sentences:

La fiesta fue ayer.
¿Fuiste a la tienda hoy?

Can you tell which sentence contains a form of the verb *ir?* If you said, *"¿Fuiste a la tienda hoy?,"* that's right!

	S E R	
	(pretérito de ser)	
fui	*(fwee)*	*I was*
fuiste	*(FWEESteh)*	*you were*
fue	*(fweh)*	*he/she/it/you (Ud). was*
fuimos	*(FWEEmos)*	*we were*
fuisteis	*(FWEEStehs)*	*y'all were*
fueron	*(FWEHron)*	*they/you (Uds.) were*

	I R	
	(pretérito de ir)	
fui	*(fwee)*	*I went*
fuiste	*(FWEESteh)*	*you went*
fue	*(fweh)*	*he/she/it/you (Ud). went*
fuimos	*(FWEEmos)*	*we went*
fuisteis	*(FWEEStehs)*	*y'all went*
fueron	*(FWEHron)*	*they/you (Uds.) went*

COMER
to eat
(pretérito de comer)

comí	*(koMEE)*	*I ate*
comiste	*(koMEESteh)*	*you ate*
comió	*(koMYO)*	*he/she/it/you (Ud). ate*
comimos	*(koMEEmos)*	*we ate*
comisteis	*(koMEESteys)*	*y'all ate*
comieron	*(koMYEHron)*	*they/you (Uds.) ate*

VIVIR
to live
(pretérito de vivir)

viví	*(beeBEE)*	*I lived*
viviste	*(beeBEESteh)*	*you lived*
vivió	*(beeBYO)*	*he/she/it/you (Ud). lived*
vivimos	*(beeBEEmos)*	*we lived*
vivisteis	*(beeBEESteys)*	*y'all lived*
vivieron	*(beeBYEHron)*	*they/you (Uds.) lived*

Now you can recognize and use lots of verbs in the *pretérito*. As you read the following paragraph, you'll notice that some of the verbs are missing. Look at the pictures and write what each person did in the blanks, using the *pretérito* forms of all the verbs.

Examples: Ayer "comí" *(I ate)* una pizza.   "Fue" *(he went)* al cine.
      yesterday

Choose one of these words to fill each space.

nadamos	fuimos	comió	llamé
miró	jugó	hablamos	pensamos

Ayer, yo _____ a mi amiga. Nosotras
      1.

_____ por mucho tiempo del fin de
    2.   semana. Me dijo que estaba
      muy cansada.

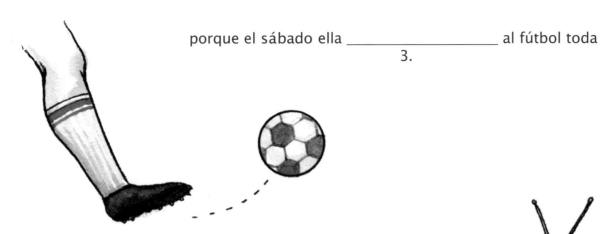

porque el sábado ella _____ al fútbol toda
3.

la mañana. Entonces se quedó en casa el domingo y

_____ televisión todo el día.
4.

Entonces me preguntó, "¿Qué hiciste tú?" Le dije que el sábado mi novio y yo

_____ en el lago.
5.

El sábado por la noche

nosotros _____ a una fiesta.
6.

CHAPTER 13

¿Qué quieres comer?
What do you want to eat?

(bwehn proBEHcho)
¡Buen provecho!
Enjoy your meal!

(saLOOTH)
¡Salud!
Cheers!

(oon POko deh)
un poco (de)
a little bit (of)/some

(meh MWEHro deh AHMbreh)
Me muero de hambre.
I'm dying of hunger.

el té
tea

el café
coffee

(sehrBEHsa)
una cerveza
a beer

(BEEno)
el vino
wine

(behBEEda)
una bebida
a beverage

(FROOta)
la fruta
fruit

(POStreh)
el postre
dessert

(FREHsas)
las fresas
strawberries

(TORta)
la torta
cake

(pasTEHL)
el pastel
pie

(PEEnya)
la piña
pineapple

(mahnSAnas)
las manzanas
apples

(sehREHsas)
las cerezas
cherries

(DOOLsehs)
los dulces
candy

(ehLAdoh)
el helado
ice cream

(bahNAHnas)
las bananas
bananas

(naRAHNhas)
las naranjas
oranges

(KARneh)
la carne
meat

(pehsKAdoh)
el pescado
fish

(POyo)
el pollo
chicken

(pahn)
el pan
bread

(haMON)
el jamón
ham

(behrDOOras)
las verduras
vegetables

(beesTEHK)
el bistec
beef

(ehnsaLAda)
la ensalada
salad

(ahRROS)
el arroz
rice

(KEHso)
el queso
cheese

(geeSAHNtehs)
los guisantes
peas

(tohMAtehs)
los tomates
tomatoes

(LEHcheh)
la leche
milk

(sehBOyas)
las cebollas
onions

(sanaOHryas)
las zanahorias
carrots

(WEHbos)
los huevos
eggs

(PApas FREEtas)
las papas fritas
French fries

(chahmpeeNYOnehs)
los champiñones
mushrooms

(SOpa)
la sopa
soup

STORY

Tres amigos están en un restaurante: Enrique, Gregorio y Roberto.

Scene 1: The three men are chatting while looking at their menus.

Enrique: ¿Qué quieres comer?

(PYEHNso pehDEER)

Gregorio: No tengo mucha hambre. Pienso pedir sopa y ensalada.
I plan to order

Enrique: ¿Y tú, Roberto?

(dehsayooNEH)

Roberto: ¿Yo? ¡Me muero de hambre! No desayuné esta mañana.
I didn't eat breakfast

Enrique: ¿De veras?¿Por qué no?

(dehspehrTEH)   *(TOObeh)*   *(yehGEH)*

Roberto: Me desperté tarde y no tuve tiempo para comer. De hecho, llegué tarde al trabajo.
I woke up   *I didn't have*

(LEEo)

Gregorio: ¡Qué lío!
What a drag!

Scene 2: The waiter comes to the table and asks for their orders.

(LEEStohs)

Mesero: ¿Están listos para pedir?
Are you ready

Gregorio: ¿Qué es la sopa del día?

(KREHma deh AHpyo)

Mesero: Hoy es crema de apio.
cream of celery

Gregorio: Bueno. Quiero sopa y una ensalada verde, por favor.

Mesero: ¿Y quiere queso parmesano en la ensalada?   **Gregorio:** Un poco, sí.

Mesero: Bien. ¿Es todo?   **Gregorio:** Sí.   **Mesero:** ¿Para Ud., Señor?

Enrique: Quisiera una tortilla de huevos con queso blanco y una ensalada de tomate.

(flahn)
Mesero: ¿Algo más?   **Enrique:** Sí. De postre quiero flan.   **Mesero:** ¿Y Ud., Señor?
Anything else?   *custard*

(beeNAYgreh)   (ahntohHEEtoh)
Roberto: Primero, quisiera los calamares al vinagre como antojito. Y para el plato
                                                              as an appetizer

 principal, el pollo en salsa de vino.
 main course

(lo SYEHNtoh)   (akaBO)   (sahlMOHN al aHEEyo)
Mesero: Lo siento, Señor. Se nos acabó el pollo. Tenemos un salmón al ajillo que es excelente.
 I'm sorry   we're out of   salmon in garlic sauce

Roberto: Bien. El salmón entonces.   **Mesero:** ¿Quiere postre?

(baiNEEya)
Roberto: Sí, el helado de vainilla, por favor.

Enrique: También quisiéramos una garrafa de vino blanco casero.
                                    carafe   house white wine

Mesero: Muy bien.

Scene 3: The friends get their food.

Enrique, Gregorio, and Roberto: ¡Salud! ¡Buen provecho!

PRACTICE

Use the English clues on the following page to find the words in Spanish.

DOWN

1. cake
2. eggs
3. cherries
4. beef
5. cheese
7. apple
8. dessert
11. ham
12. meat
13. wine

ACROSS

4. beverage
6. vegetables
9. ice cream
10. rice
14. french fries
15. chicken

REVIEW

¿Cierto o falso?

1. Roberto tiene mucha hambre. _____

2. El flan es un postre. _____

3. Enrique pidió vino tinto. _____

4. Roberto va a comer pollo. _____

5. Roberto quiere el helado de chocolate. _____

CHAPTER 14

¿Qué te pasa?
What's the matter?

(agoTAda)
Estoy agotada.
I'm exhausted.

(atareaDEEseema)
Estoy atareadísima.
I'm swamped.

(fehLEES coomplehAHnyos)
¡Feliz cumpleaños!
Happy Birthday!

No me siento bien.
I don't feel well.

VOCABULARY

(sehlehBRAR)	*(rehsFRYAHdoh)*	*(ehnFEHRmo/a)*	*(saLOOTH)*	*(PEHso)*
celebrar	un resfriado	enfermo/a	la salud	el peso
celebrate	*a cold*	*sick*	*health*	*weight*

DIALOG

(EENteemas) (ehnKWEHNtran) (almorSAR)
Unas amigas íntimas se encuentran para almorzar en casa de Sara para celebrar el
    close   *meet*   *to eat lunch*

cumpleaños de Cristina.

Sara: Hola, Cristina. ¡Feliz cumpleaños!

Cristina: Hola, Sara. ¡Gracias! Hace muy buen tiempo hoy.

                         (AYreh LEEbreh)
                   ¡Oh! ¿Vamos a comer al aire libre?
                           outdoors

Sara: ¡Sí! En el jardín.

Julia: Hola.

Sara: Julia, ¿qué te pasa?

Julia: No me siento bien.

         (LAHSteema)
Sara: Ay, ¡qué lástima! ¿Tienes un resfriado?
         what a shame

               (DWEHleh)(garGANta)
Julia: Creo que sí. Me duele la garganta y estoy agotada. No tengo ganas de
       I think so.   *I have a sore throat*   *I don't feel like*

         trabajar. De hecho, No voy a volver al trabajo esta tarde.
                   I'm not going to go back

Sara: ¿Cuánto tiempo hace que estás enferma?
         How long have you been sick?

Julia: Como dos días.   **Sara:**   ¿Por qué viniste hoy?
                                             did you come

Julia: ¡Es el cumpleaños de Cristina! ¡Quiero ayudarla a celebrar!
                                    to help her

Cristina: *(aMAbleh)*
Eres muy amable, Julia. Gracias.
that's very nice of you

Julia: De todos modos, ¿cómo estás, Cristina? Estabas tan enferma el mes pasado.
anyway   you were   so

Cristina: Estoy bien ahora. ¡Mira! Aumenté de peso. También, ando en bicicleta al
I gained weight.

trabajo todos los días.

Julia: *(marabeeYOsaMEHNteh)*
Eso es fantástico. Te ves maravillosamente. ¿Cómo te va el trabajo?
that   You look wonderful.   How's work going?

Cristina: Al momento me encuentro atareadísima, pero es muy interesante.
I find myself

(koNOSko)
Conozco a personas diferentes todos los días.
I meet

Julia: ¡Qué chévere!
How cool!

84

Sara: *(BEHNgan)*
Bueno, ¡el almuerzo está listo! ¡Vengan a comer!
Come eat!

Hay una ensalada de pollo, piña fresca, unos tamales de chile verde, y
fresh

(freeHOlehs)
arroz con frijoles negros. Y de postre, tenemos una torta de coco con
beans   *coconut*

(chamPAnya)
fresas Empecemos con una copa de champaña.
Let's start with a glass of champagne!

Julia, Cristina, Sara: ¡Salud!

Julia, Sara: ¡Al cumpleaños número cuarenta de Cristina!

Cristina: ¡Y a la salud de Julia!

(mehHOR)
Julia: Ya, me siento mejor.
already   better

¿Sí o No?

Read *en inglés*. Answer *en español*.

_____   1. Does Julia have a sore throat?

_____   2. Does Cristina like her job?

_____   3. Is the celebration at Julia's house?

_____   4. Is it Cristina's thirtieth birthday?

_____   5. Was Cristina sick last month?

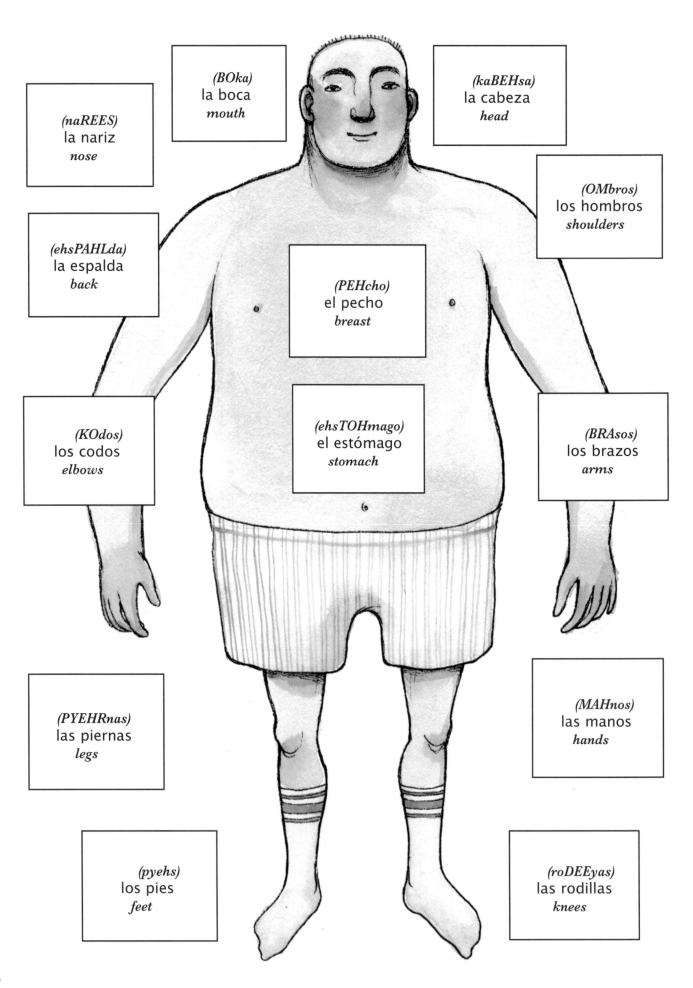

(naREES)
la nariz
nose

(BOka)
la boca
mouth

(kaBEHsa)
la cabeza
head

(OMbros)
los hombros
shoulders

(ehsPAHLda)
la espalda
back

(PEHcho)
el pecho
breast

(KOdos)
los codos
elbows

(ehsTOHmago)
el estómago
stomach

(BRAsos)
los brazos
arms

(PYEHRnas)
las piernas
legs

(MAHnos)
las manos
hands

(pyehs)
los pies
feet

(roDEEyas)
las rodillas
knees

PRACTICE

Remember that Julia said, *Me duele la garganta.* See if you can match *el inglés* with *el español* by looking at the diagram. Write the letters in the blanks.

1. Me duele el estómago. _____
2. Me duele la rodilla. _____
3. Me duele la cabeza. _____
4. Me duelen los pies. _____
5. Me duele la oreja. _____
6. Me duelen los ojos. _____
7. Me duele el cuello. _____
8. Me duele la espalda. _____

a. My feet hurt.
b. My eyes hurt.
c. I have a stomachache.
d. My back hurts.
e. My neck hurts.
f. My knee hurts.
g. I have a headache.
h. I have an earache.

FOCUS

Do you remember the preterit from Chapter 12? The verb *venir* is irregular in the preterit; here are its forms:

VENIR *(pretérito)*
to come

vine	*(BEEneh)*	*I came*
viniste	*(beeNEESteh)*	*you came*
vino	*(BEEno)*	*he/she/it/you (Ud). came*
vinimos	*(beeNEEmos)*	*we came*
vinisteis	*(beeNEEstehys)*	*y'all came*
vinieron	*(beeNYEHrohn)*	*they/you (Uds.) came*

In Chapter 1, you learned the reflexive verb *llamarse*, to call oneself. A reflexive verb, grammatically speaking, is a verb whose <u>subject</u> and <u>object</u> are the same individual(s). In English, special pronouns like myself, himself, yourselves, etc. are used to indicate reflexive action. Sometimes Spanish reflexive verbs can be easily translated with an English reflexive, but it is important to remember that the English equivalent of many reflexive verbs in Spanish <u>isn't</u> reflexive. *Sentirse* is one example; usually the best English translation for this verb is "to feel".

SENTIRSE
to feel (emotions)

me siento	*(meh SYEHNtoh)*	*I feel*
te sientes	*(tch SYEHNtchs)*	*you feel*
se siente	*(seh SYEHNteh)*	*he/she/it/you (Ud). feels*
nos sentimos	*(nos sehnTEEmos)*	*we feel*
os sentís	*(os sehnTEES)*	*y'all feel*
se sienten	*(seh SYEHNtehn)*	*they/you (Uds.) feel*

CHAPTER 15

(KEHda)
¡Eso te queda muy bien!
That looks great on you!

(no teh preoKOOpehs)
¡No te preocupes!
Don't worry!

(olBEEdalo)
¡Olvídalo!
No way!

(ehn BEHNta)
en venta
on sale

VOCABULARY

(BAnyo)
el traje de baño
bathing suit

(peeHAma)
el pijama
pajamas

(TEHnees)
los zapatos de tenis
tennis shoes

(kameeSEHta)
la camiseta
t-shirt

(BAta)
la bata
bathrobe

(BOtas)
las botas
boots

los bluejeans
jeans

(pahnTOOflas)
las pantuflas
slippers

(sosTEHN)
el sostén
bra

(soodaDEHra)
la sudadera
sweatshirt

(kombeenaSYON)
la combinación (de mujer)
suit

(kalsohnSEEyos)
los calzoncillos
underwear

un sombrero
hat

(booFAHNda)
una bufanda
scarf

(behsTEEdoh)
un vestido
dress

(chaKEHta)
una chaqueta
jacket

(aBREEgo)
un abrigo

(MEHdyas)
unas medias
panty hose

(GWAHNtehs)
unos guantes
gloves

(TRAheh)
un traje
suit

unos
zapatos
shoes

(korBAta)
una corbata

(eempehrmeeABleh)
un impermeable
rain jacket

(kalsehTEEnehs)
unos calcetines
socks

(paRAgwas)
un paraguas
umbrella

DIALOG

(HORheh)   (seewataNEHho)
Jorge y María González piensan ir a Zihuatanejo de vacaciones. Van de compras para
                                                                    they're shopping

(konsehGEER ROpa aproPYAda)(aoREEta)
conseguir ropa apropiada. Ahorita están en una tienda de ropa para hombres. Jorge se
  to get   *clothing*   *right now*

(PRWEHba)
prueba un traje gris.
is trying on

                    (SEERbeh)   (traEHR)(neenGOON)
María: Ese traje te sirve bien, pero yo no voy a traer ningún traje.
            that   *fits you*   *to bring any*

            (tahl behs)   (EHSteh)
Jorge: Tal vez tienes razón. Éste es demasiado formal para Zihuatanejo.
            maybe   *this*

            (POHNteh)(EHStos)   (EHSta)
María: Ponte estos pantalones blancos y esta camisa rosada.
             try on *these*   *this*

                              (DAmeh)
Jorge: ¿Rosada? ¡De ninguna manera! Dame una camisa azul, por favor.
                              give me

Dependiente: ¿Cómo lo puedo ayudar, Señor?

Jorge: ¿Tiene esta camisa en azul?

                        (taMAHnyo)
Dependiente: ¿Del mismo tamaño?
                  In the same size?

Jorge: Sí.

Dependiente: Aquí está.

                        (BOOSko)
Jorge: Mucho mejor. También busco una chaqueta deportiva.
                        I'm looking for

Dependiente: Ésta está en venta.
                  this one
                        (KEHda)
María: Está muy de moda. Ay, ¡te queda muy bien, amor!
            It's very stylish   *It looks great on you, sweetheart*

Jorge: Bueno. Me gustaría comprar los pantalones, la camisa, y la chaqueta.

(PAgehlos ehn aKEHya KAha)
Dependiente: Muy bien. Páguelos en aquella caja, por favor.
Pay for them at that register over there, please.

Ahora Jorge y María están en una tienda de ropa para mujeres.

María se prueba un vestido amarillo.

(LEENdoh)   *(LARgo)*
Jorge: Ese vestido es lindo, pero te queda demasiado largo.
      pretty   *long*

(pehKEHnyo)
María: Puede ser... Señorita, ¿tiene éste en un tamaño más pequeño?
                                     smaller

Dependiente: No, Señora, éste no lo tenemos en ese tamaño.
                             that

Jorge: Mira este vestido rojo, amor.

(oRREEbleh)   *(yeBAR)*
María: ¡Ese vestido es horrible! No puedo llevar ése.
                     wear

Jorge: No te preocupes. ¡A mí no me gusta tampoco!
                          either

Dependiente: ¿Le gusta esta falda, Señora? Es la última y es de su tamaño.

(OOLteema)

the last one

María: ¡Me gusta mucho esa falda!

(PRWEHbala)

Jorge: ¡Pruébala!

Try it on!

Dependiente: Aquí está una blusa amarilla y una bufanda de seda que podría

(SEHda)   (poDREEa)

silk   you could

llevar con la falda.

(paREHseh)

María: Bueno....¿Qué te parece?   **Jorge:** ¡Te queda muy bien!

What do you think?

(pwehs)(BAmonos)

María: ¡Bueno pues! Vámonos a buscar trajes de baño. ¡Luego estaremos listos para Zihuatanejo!

Well then!   let's go   *we'll be*

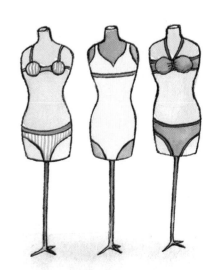

¿COMPRENDES?

Which of these statements describe the situations in the dialogs? Put a check next to the sentences that are true.

1. _____ Jorge compra una camisa rosada.

2. _____ A María le gusta la falda.

3. _____ Jorge se pone un impermeable.

4. _____ Jorge y María piensan ir a Zihuatanejo.

5. _____ Jorge dice que el vestido amarillo es demasiado corto.

Each of the 5 words below is a scrambled word for a piece of women's clothing. Unscramble each of the clue words. Copy the letters in the numbered cells to other cells with the same number. Then you will find the answer to the question! (The answer does not refer to the dialogs in this chapter. This is just to practice some of the new words you learned.)

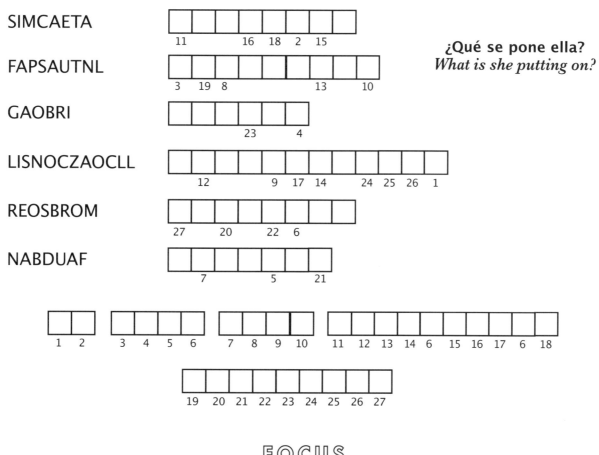

SIMCAETA

11 16 18 2 15

FAPSAUTNL

3 19 8 13 10

GAOBRI

23 4

LISNOCZAOCLL

12 9 17 14 24 25 26 1

REOSBROM

27 20 22 6

NABDUAF

7 5 21

¿Qué se pone ella?
What is she putting on?

1 2   3 4 5 6   7 8 9 10   11 12 13 14 6 15 16 17 6 18

19 20 21 22 23 24 25 26 27

FOCUS

THIS, THAT, THESE, THOSE

Words like this, these, that, those are "demonstrative adjectives". In English, there are singular and plural forms of these adjectives, and they indicate two different degrees of "closeness" to the speaker. This and these are used to refer to things that are physically or metaphorically "closer", while the forms that and those indicate things that are farther away in space or time.

Spanish has more forms of the demonstrative adjectives than English. As you might expect, demonstrative adjectives in Spanish, in addition to singular and plural forms, come in masculine and feminine forms as well. Like other adjectives in Spanish, the demonstrative adjectives agree in gender and number with the nouns they modify. In addition, Spanish demonstrative adjectives identify <u>three</u> degrees of closeness to the speaker: close, far, and farther. These are the forms of *los adjetivos demostrativos* (demonstrative adjectives) in Spanish:

Este, esta, estos, estas: this/these
Ese, esa, esos, esas: that/those
Aquel, aquella, aquellos, aquellas: that/those over there

CHAPTER 16

(aSEE ehs la BEEtha)
¡Así es la vida!
That's life!

No matter how much *te preparas* for *un viaje* to a foreign country, there will often be some unexpected things that can happen. When some of these things are unfortunate or unpleasant, it helps to know some of the *lenguaje* in order to *comprender* what people (like *médicos* or *policías*) are asking. *Tú* might *también necesitar explicar* what happened. A good attitude goes a long way in *prepararte* to cope with unfortunate circumstances. Accepting an unforeseen event as part of *tu experiencia* will help you get through it. You will see in the story in this chapter how Roberto, from New York, handles his *problemas* on a business trip to Buenos Aires.

(keh oRROR)
¡Qué horror!
What a terrible thing!

(mehHOR TARdeh keh NOONka)
¡Mejor tarde que nunca!
Better late than never!

VOCABULARY

(pahnTAyah)
la pantalla
screen

(fax)
fax
fax

(eemprehSORah)
la impresora
printer

(tehLEHfono)
el teléfono
telephone

(kompootaDOHra)
la computadora
computer

(tehLEHfono sehlooLAR)
el teléfono celular
cell phone

(tehkLAHdo)
el teclado
keyboard

(rahtOHN)
el ratón
mouse

STORY

(paSO)   *(BYAheh) (BWEHnos Ayrehs)*
Lee lo que le pasó a Roberto en un viaje a Buenos Aires.
read   *what happened to*

(EEso)
Mi hermano Roberto no tiene suerte. Hizo un viaje a Buenos Aires el mes pasado.
                    he took a trip

(porTAteel) *(roBO)*   *(aehroPWEHRtoh)*
Primero, su computadora portátil se robó en el aeropuerto. ¡Qué horror!
       laptop   *was stolen*

(eentehnTOH)   *(HEHfeh)* *(rehseeBYO)*
Entonces, intentó mandar un fax a su oficina en Nueva York, pero su jefe no lo recibió.
       he tried   *boss   didn't receive it*

(ehnsaiYO)   *(dehHAR)(mehnSAheh)*   *(Makeena kontehstaDOHra)*
Después, Roberto ensayó con dejar un mensaje en la máquina contestadora en su trabajo,
       tried to   *leave a message*   *the answering machine*

(foonsyoNAba)   *(yehGO)*
pero no funcionaba. El día después de que llegó a Buenos Aires,
   it wasn't working   *after*   *he arrived*

(POOso)   *(pehrDYO)*
Roberto se puso de muy mal humor porque se perdió y llegó 40 minutos tarde
       got into a really bad mood because

para su primera reunión.

95

(DEEho)   *(seenTYO)*

(cuando alguien en la reunión le dijo, "¡Mejor tarde que nunca!, se sintió un poco mejor.)
someone   *he felt*

Por lo menos Roberto llegó a mandar unos correos electrónicos a su jefe, a su familia
at least   *succeeded in sending*

(ehnkonTRO) (seebehrkaFEH)   *(aSEE)*   *(ooSAba)*

(como a mí), y a unos amigos. Encontró un cibercafé cerca de su hotel, así que usaba las
                    he found   *so*   *he would use*

(aYA)(KAsee)   *(aBEEa)*

computadoras allá casi todas las noches. Mi hermano dijo que siempre había mucha
there almost   *said*   *there was*

(HEHNteh)

gente en el café que mandaba correos electrónicos, navegaba la red, y usaba el
people

(prosehsaDOR deh TEHKStos)

procesador de textos. Sin embargo, Roberto no pudo teclear muy rápido porque el
word processor

                                              (DWEHnyo)

teclado era diferente. Una noche, derramó café en el ratón y el teclado; y el dueño no
                                                 the owner

(ehsTOObo)

estuvo muy contento. ¡Qué horror!
wasn't

Entonces el sábado por la mañana, hacía sol y Roberto alquiló un coche para conducir al

(alkeeLO) — rented
(kondooSEER) — to drive

campo para un picnic al lado del río. Desafortunadamente (pero no sorprendentemente)

(KAHMpo) — countryside
(dehsafortooNAdaMEHnteh) — unfortunately
(sorprehnDEHNtehMEHnteh) — surprisingly

su coche se le paró en la carretera. El domingo, alquiló una bicicleta para andar a un

(karrehTEHra) — broke down / highway

parque grande. Llovía casi todo el tiempo y mientras regresaba tuvo un reventón.

(yoBEEa) — it was raining
(TOObo oon rehbehnTOHN) — on the way home — he had a flat

¡Pobre Roberto! Sin embargo, aun cuando no

even

tiene suerte, mi hermano siempre dice,

"¡Así es la vida!".

¿COMPRENDES?

Match the phrases on the left with the words on the right.

_____	1. ¡Mejor tarde que nunca!	a) el ratón y el teclado
_____	2. el jefe no recibió	b) el cibercafé
_____	3. se le paró en la carretera	c) la reunión
_____	4. derramó el café en	d) la computadora portátil
_____	5. tuvo un reventón	e) el coche
_____	6. mandó correos electrónicos de	f) la bicicleta
_____	7. se robó	g) el fax

MATCHING

See if you can match the past tense verb with the meaning. Look back at the story for help.

_____	1. encontró	a) rented
_____	2. alquiló	b) was stolen
_____	3. perdió	c) tried
_____	4. dijo	d) found
_____	5. recibió	e) lost
_____	6. llegó	f) said
_____	7. se robó	g) arrived
_____	8. derramó	h) received
_____	9. intentó	i) spilled

FOCUS

The quality of police service varies widely throughout the Spanish-speaking world. In some places the police might be very helpful to you if you have a problem; in others, they might be polite but not so helpful. In some places you might be expected to contribute monetarily to the police, and it's possible that contacting the police in some locations could actually be dangerous to you.

If you are lucky enough to know some of the locals, ask them what they think about the police and whom you should contact in an emergency. When in doubt, it's usually a better idea to contact the embassy or consulate of your home country in legal or monetary emergencies or if any of your identification is lost or stolen. Remember that in many situations, the hotel reception desk can be very helpful, and is often a good place to start or to get advice on how to proceed.

(ehmehrHEHNsya)
una emergencia
an emergency

(soKOrro)
¡Socorro!
Help!

(laDRON)
¡Ladrón!
Thief!

(keh paSO)
¿Qué pasó?
What happened?

(meh roBAron)
Me robaron el(la)…
They stole my…

(pehrDEE)
Perdí mi(s)…
I've lost my…

Find these 5 emergency words in the puzzle:

emergencia, incendio, ladrón, policía, socorro.

v	t	l	j	e	x	i	t	d	a	l	u	s	n	b
i	n	c	e	n	d	i	o	i	a	l	r	l	h	j
l	m	f	m	q	j	r	c	d	m	g	b	d	l	j
v	t	d	g	t	o	n	r	e	q	d	y	t	x	n
n	c	e	y	n	e	ó	h	c	h	t	i	h	z	a
o	q	c	r	g	n	e	j	h	t	a	u	o	t	s
p	s	t	r	l	b	u	b	j	q	t	p	q	i	o
r	o	e	g	h	m	c	s	s	b	d	h	u	x	o
o	m	l	s	a	n	t	o	c	n	l	b	f	h	d
e	i	q	i	i	c	j	c	d	i	n	q	h	f	r
o	p	e	i	c	m	k	o	a	z	z	a	o	v	m
p	p	o	y	k	í	c	r	r	c	v	i	p	n	b
i	q	o	u	p	o	a	r	u	h	a	a	l	m	d
t	j	t	o	g	a	m	o	p	t	v	d	j	h	v
p	x	c	j	o	q	f	f	k	b	n	b	c	r	r

¡Felicidades! Be sure to use the accompanying "phrase" stickers to practice what you've learned. Place them around your work and home. Build on the foundation this book provides by immersing yourself in Spanish as much as you can. Spanish radio and television programs may be available in your area. Spanish films are another enjoyable way to hear the language. Read anything you can find in Spanish, including children's books, easy novels, comics, magazines, newspapers, and even the labels on household products. Search the Internet for Spanish websites that will give you countless opportunities to read and listen to Spanish.

ANSWER KEY

CHAPTER 1

Practice

1. ¿ <u>dónde</u> quiere usted tomar <u>cena</u> ?

2. ¿ Dónde <u>quiere</u> <u>usted</u> tomar <u>desayuno</u> ?

3. ¿ Dónde quiere usted <u>tomar</u> <u>almuerzo</u> ?

4. ¿ <u>dónde</u> quiere usted comer ?

Matching

1. a   2. f   3. c   4. b   5. e   6. d

CHAPTER 2

Number Practice

1. cuatro   2. diez   3. cinco   4. tres
5. uno   6. siete   7. ocho   8. nueve

Practice

1. Ana y su amiga comen en un restaurante.
2. Julia tiene dos sandwiches.
3. Juan entra en el restaurante.
4. Juan está muy contento.

CHAPTER 3

Dialog Practice

1. ¿Cuántos años tienes?
2. ¿De dónde es Ud.?
3. ¿ Cómo se llama (Ud.)?
4. ¿Es Ud. española?

Focus – Asking questions in Spanish

1. ¿Es Ud. americano?
2. ¿Tienes hambre?
3. ¿Vosotros tenéis hambre?
4. ¿De dónde son Uds.?
5. ¿ Tú comes carne?
6. ¿Cuántos años tienes tú?

CHAPTER 4

Do you understand?

1. Carmen is española.
2. The clerk speaks too rapidly.
3. He wants to buy two apple fritters.
4. Carmen asks for mineral water.
5. This scene takes place in a bakery.

Practice: ¿Cómo le puedo servir?

1. once	2. dieciocho	3. quince
4. tres	5. cinco	6. dos

CHAPTER 5

Practice

1. casa (house)	2. años (years)	3. simpático (nice)	
4. graciosa (funny)	5. trabajo (work/job)	6. tren (train)	7. coche (car)

Crossword Puzzle : los Colores

Across:

5. anaranjado

6. gris

7. negro

8. rosado

Down:

1. verde

2. blanco

3. rojo

4. marrón

5. amarillo

Practice

3 miércoles	7 domingo	2 martes	5 viernes
1 lunes	6 sábado	4 jueves	

CHAPTER 6

¿Quién ganó la carrera?

A is primero	F is sexto
B is segundo	G is séptimo
C is tercero	H is octavo
D is cuarto	I is noveno
E is quinto	J is décimo

CHAPTER 7

Practice – Translating picture captions

1. The mother is at the beach in the summertime.
2. The father is in the mountains in the winter.
3. The brother takes a walk through the forest in the autumn.
4. The sisters pick up the flowers in the spring.

Practice

English to Spanish
1. Tengo veinte años.
2. Le gustan los colores de otoño (anaranjado, rojo, amarillo, y marrón).
3. ¡A mí también! A Mercedes y a mí nos encantan las flores bellas.
4. En junio, julio y agosto a menudo vamos a la playa.

Focus: Noun Gender Practice

1. la hermana	2. la playa	3. la familia	4. el queso
5. el coche	6. el hombre	7. la mañana	8. la estación
9. el museo	10. la calle		

CHAPTER 8

This is my family

3. a) Rodolfo
   b) el padre
	4. a) Sofia
	   b) la madre
		5. a) Amalia
		   b) la esposa	

8. a) Natalia
   b) la hija
	7. a) Alberto
	   b) el suegro
		6. a) Elena
		   b) la suegra
			1. a) Patricio
			   b) el hermano

2. a) Marina b) la cuñada			

A. Ciertas o falsas

1. f   2. f   3. c   4. c   5. c   6. c   7. f

¿Quién?   Fill-in-the-blanks

1. Amalia   2. Sofia   3. Patricio   4. Natalia   5. Pedro

Practice : Adjectives

1. la mujer alta	2. la hija baja	3. los hombres españoles
4. la abuela trabajadora	5. la sobrina inteligente	6. los padres inteligentes

CHAPTER 9

¿Comprendes?

1. Elisa tiene frío.
2. Elisa está en Alaska.
3. Está lloviendo en Quito.
4. Trabaja todos los días excepto los Domingos.
5. Quiere visitar Alaska en el verano.

More Practice:

La hija	Mamá
2,3,5,7,8	1,4,6

¿Qué tiempo hace?

1. hace calor   2. llueve mucho   3. hace muy mal tiempo
4. nieva   5. hace viento   6. está húmedo   7. hace (muy) buen tiempo

Practice and Review

1. verano   2. frío   3. mucho   4. aquí   5. primavera

CHAPTER 10

¿Comprendes?

1. falso   2. cierto   3. falso   4. falso   5. cierto

¿Qué hora es?

1. d   2. e   3. a   4. c   5. b

CHAPTER 11

¿Comprendes?

1. D   2. C   3. E   4. B   5. A

Focus

1. en   2. en/sobre   3. en/sobre   4. detrás de   5. debajo de   6. al lado de

Write two sentences

Possible answers:
1. Hay un libro (una novela) en la alfombra.
2. El perro está sobre la alfombra.

CHAPTER 12

Matching

1. f   2. e   3. d   4. a   5. c   6. b

Practice

1. llamé
2. hablamos
3. jugó
4. miró
5. nadamos
6. fuimos

CHAPTER 13

Practice: La Comida

Across:

4. bebida
6. verduras
9. helado
10. arroz
14. papas fritas
15. pollo

Down:

1. torta
2. huevos
3. cerezas
4. bistek
5. queso
7. manzana
8. postre
11. jamón
12. carne
13. vino

¿Cierto o falso?

1. cierto   2. cierto   3. falso – pidió vino blanco
4. falso – va a comer salmón   5. falso – quiere vainilla

CHAPTER 14

¿Sí o No?

1. sí   2. sí   3. no (está en casa de Sara)   4. no (es el cuarenta)   5. sí

Practice

1. c   2. f   3. g   4. a   5. h   6. b   7. e   8. d

CHAPTER 15

¿Comprendes?

1. F   2. T   3. F   4.T   5. F

Scrambled words:

camiseta
pantuflas
abrigo
calzoncillos
sombrero
bufanda

Answer:

Se pone unos calcetines amarillos.

CHAPTER 16

¿Comprendes?

1. c   2. g   3. e   4. a   5. f   6. b   7. d

Matching: Verbs

1. d   2. a   3. e   4. f   5. h   6. g   7. b   8. i   9. c

GLOSSARY

Spanish-English

A

a – at
a la vez – at the same time
a menudo – often
a pesar de – in spite of
A ver – let's see
abajo – downstairs
abierto – open
el abrigo – coat
abril – April
la abuela – grandmother
el abuelo – grandfather
aburrido – bored
acabarse – to come to an end
afuera – outside
agosto – August
agotado – exhausted
el agua (f) – water
ahora – now
ahorita – right now
al aire libre – outdoors
¡Al contrario! – On the contrary!
al lado de – next to
al otro lado (de) – on the other side (of)
la alfombra – rug
algo – something
allá – (over) there
el almacén – department store
almorzar (ue) – to have lunch
el almuerzo – lunch
alquilar – to rent
alto – tall (person)
amable – kind, nice
amarillo/a – yellow
el/la amigo/a – friend
el amor – love
anaranjado – orange
andar – to go; to walk
andén – track
anoche – last night
anteayer – the day before yesterday
el antojito – appetizer
el año – year
aparecer – to appear
el apio – celery
aquél – that one over there
aquel – that over there
aquella – that over there

aquélla – that one over there
aquello – that (thing) over there (neuter)
aquéllos/as – those ones over there
aquellos/as – those over there
aquí – here
arriba – upstairs
¡Arriba los corazones! – Keep your chin up!
el arroz – rice
así – so
asombroso – amazing
atareadísimo – swamped
atrasado – late
aún – even
el avión – plane
ayer – yesterday
azul – blue

B

bajo – short (person)
las bananas – bananas
el baño – bathroom
¡Basta! – That's enough!
bastante – enough
la bata – bathrobe
la bebida – beverage
bello/a – beautiful
bien – well
billete – ticket
el bistec – steak
blanco/a – white
la blusa – blouse
la boca – mouth
el boleto – ticket
el bolígrafo – pen
la bolsa – purse
el bosque – forest; woods
las botas – boots
la botella – bottle
el brazo – arm
buen(o) – good
¡Buen provecho! – Enjoy your meal!
la bufanda – scarf
los buñuelos – fritters

C

la cabeza – head
el café – coffee
la caja – box, cash box
los calcetines – socks
el calor – heat
la calle – street

los calzoncillos – underpants
la cama – bed
caminar – to travel
la camisa – shirt
la camiseta – undershirt
el campo – countryside
canoso – gray-haired
cansado – tired
¡Caramba! – Darn!
la carne – meat
la carretera – highway
la casa – house
casarse – to get married
casero – domestic
casi – almost
castaño – chestnut brown
catorce – fourteen
la cebolla – onion
celebrar – to celebrate
la cena – dinner
cerca de – nearby
las cerezas – cherries
cero – zero
cerrado – closed
la cerveza – beer
cien – one hundred
cierto – true
cinco – five
cincuenta – fifty
el cine – cinema
la ciudad – city
¡Claro que no! – Of course not
¡Claro que sí! – Certainly!
el coco – coconut
el coche – the car
cocinar – to cook
el cocinero – cook
el codo – elbow
la cola – line, queue
colérico – quick-tempered
la combinación (de mujer) – slip
comer – to eat
la comida – food
cómo – how
cómodo – comfortable
comprender – to understand
con el canto de lo gallos – at the crack of dawn
conducir – to drive
conmigo – with me
conocer – to be familiar with / to meet
conseguir – to get
contento – happy

la copa – wineglass
la corbata – necktie
correr – to run
corto – short
creer – to think
cruzar – to cross
cual – which
cuando – when
cuanto – how much
¿Cuánto cuesta? – How much does it cost?
cuarenta – forty
cuarto – a quarter
cuarto (4to) – fourth
cuatro – four
el cuello – neck
el cuerpo – body
el cuñado – brother-in-law

D

dar (irreg.) to give
dar miedo – to frighten
de – from/of
de hecho – in fact
de ida – one-way
de ida y vuelta – round-trip
de moda – stylish
de nada – you're welcome
¡De ninguna manera! – No way!
de todos modos – anyway
¿De veras? – Really?
de venta – on sale
debajo – underneath
décimo (10mo) – tenth
decir (irreg.) – to say
el dedo – finger
los dedos del pie – toes
demasiado – too (much)
dentro de – inside
el dependiente – clerk
el deporte – sport; game
el derecho – right
derramar – to spill
desafortunadamente – unfortunately
desayunar – to eat breakfast
el desayuno – breakfast
despertarse – to wake up
después – afterward
detrás de – behind
el día – day
diciembre – December
diecinueve – nineteen

dieciocho – eighteen
dieciséis – sixteen
diecisiete – seventeen
los dientes – teeth
diez – ten
¡Dios mío! – My goodness!
disfrutar – to enjoy
divertido – fun, entertaining
doce – twelve
doler (ue) – to hurt
domingo – Sunday
donde – where
dormir (ue) – to sleep
dos – two
el dueño – owner
los dulces – candy

E

él – he/ it, masculine
el – the, masculine
ella – she/ it, feminine
ellas – they, feminine
ellos – they, masculine
empezar a – to begin
en – in, on
en mi opinión – in my opinion
en otras palabras – in other words
encantar – to enchant
encenderse (ie) – to turn on
encontrar(ue) – to meet
enero – January
enfermo/a – sick
enfrente de – in front of
la ensalada – salad
ensayar – to try; to test
entonces – then
entrar – to enter
entre – between
epicúreo – gourmet
ese – that
ese/a – that
ése/a – that one
eso – that (thing, neuter)
esos/as – those
ésos/as – those ones
los espaguetis – pasta
la espalda – back
español/a – Spanish
la esposa – wife
el esposo – husband
esquiar – to ski
la estación – season
el estado – state
los Estados Unidos –

U.S.A.
las estampillas – stamps
estar – to be
esta – this
este – this
ésta – this one
éste this one
el estómago – stomach
esto – this (thing, neuter)
estos/as – these
éstos/as – these ones
¡Estoy harto! – I've had enough!
la estrella – star
estupendo – super, fantastic, incredible

F

la falda – skirt
falso – false
febrero – February
¡Feliz cumpleaños! – Happy Birthday!
la fiesta – party
el fin de semana – weekend
la(s) flor(es) – flower(s)
francamente – frankly
frente a – facing
las fresas – strawberries
fresco – fresh
los frijoles – beans
el frío – cold
la fruta – fruit
¡Fue estupendo! – It was great!
el fútbol – soccer

G

el gato – cat
ganar – to gain; to earn
la garganta – throat
la gente – people
gracias – thanks
gracioso/a – humorous
grande – big; large
gris – gray
gritar – to shout, to yell
los guantes – gloves
guapo – handsome
los guisantes – peas
gustar – to please

H

hablar – to speak
hacer (irreg.) – to make/to do

el hambre (f) – hunger
¡Hasta luego! – see you later
hay – there is/there are
el helado – ice cream
la hermana – sister
el hermano – brother
la hija – daughter
el hijo – son
hola – hello
el hombre – man
el hombro – shoulder
la hora – the time
el horno – oven
hoy – today
los huevos – eggs

I

igualmente – likewise
el impermeable – raincoat
¡Incendio! – Fire!
el inglés – English(lang.)
íntimo – close
las investigaciones – research
el invierno – winter
ir (irreg.) – to go
la izquierda – left

J

el jamón – ham
el jardín – garden
el jefe – boss
joven – young
jueves – Thursday
jugar (ue) – to play (sports/games)
los juguetes – toys
julio – July
junio – June
junto/a (os/as) – together

L

la – the, feminine
¡Ladrón! – Thief!
el lago – lake
largo – long, length
la leche – milk
lavarse – to wash (oneself)
le – to him/her/it/you (Ud.)
leer – to read
lejos – far
lentamente – slowly
les – to them/you (Uds.)

levantarse – to get up
libre – free
lindo/a – pretty
listo/a – ready
lo/la – it
lunes – Monday

LL

llamar – to telephone
llamarse – to be called
llegar – to arrive
llevar – to bring
llover – to rain
la lluvia – rain

M

madre – mother
mal – badly
mal(o) – bad
la maleta – suitcase
mandar – to send
mandar correo electrónico – send e-mail
mañana – tomorrow
la mañana – morning
la mano – hand
la manzana – apple
el mapa – map
marrón – brown
martes – Tuesday
marzo – March
más – more
me – (to) me
Me da igual. – I don't care.
¡Me estás bromeando! – You're kidding!
Me voy. – I'm outta here.
media – half
las medias – stockings
la medianoche – midnight
el mediodía – noon
mejor – better
el mes – month
mi/s – my
el miedo – fear
mientras – while
miércoles – Wednesday
mirar – to watch
mismo – same
el montón – a ton
mucho – a lot
¡Mucho gusto! – Pleased to meet you.
muy – very

N

nadar – to swim
los naipes – (playing) cards
la naranja – orange
la nariz – nose
navegar la red – surf the Web
necesitar – to need
el negocio – affair; business
negro – black
la nieta – granddaughter
nieto – grandson
la nieve – snow
ningún/ninguna – none; nobody
No hay de que. – Don't mention it.
¡No importa! – Never mind!
¡No me digas! – No way!
la noche – night
nos – to us
nosotros/as – we
noveno (9no) – ninth
noventa – ninety
la novia – girlfriend
noviembre – November
el novio – boyfriend
nuestro/a (os/as) – our
nueve – nine
nuevo/a – new
nunca – never

O

ochenta – eighty
ocho – eight
octavo (8vo) – eighth
octubre – October
ocupado(a) – busy
ocuparse – to occupy
el ojo – eye
¡Olvídalo! – No way!
once – eleven
la oreja – ear
os – to y'all (vosotros)
el otoño – autumn
otra vez – again

P

el padre – father
los padres – parents
pagar – to pay
el pan – bread
el pan dulce – sweet roll, bun
panadería – bakery

los pantalones – pants
los pantalones cortos – shorts
las pantuflas – slippers
las papas fritas – French fries
el paraguas – umbrella
para – for, in order to
parar – to stop
pararse – to come to a standstill
el parque – park
pasado mañana – day after tomorrow
pasar – to pass
el paseo – walk; stroll
el pastel – pie
el pecho – chest
pedir – to ask for
pensar (ie) – to think
pequeño – small
perderse – to get lost
¡Perdón! – Excuse me!
pero – but
el perro – dog
el pescado – fish
el peso – weight
el pie – foot
el pijama – pajamas
el piso – floor
el plato – plate
pobre – poor
poco – little
poder – to be able
¡Policía! – Police!
el pollo – chicken
poner – to put
por – for, by, through
por favor – please
¡Por supuesto! – Of course!
portátil – portable
el postre – dessert
preferir (ie) – to prefer
preguntarse – to ask
presentar – to introduce
primero (1ro) – first
primero – first
probar (ue) to test; to try
el/la programador/a – computer programmer
pronto – soon
propio – one's own
el próximo – next
el puente – bridge
pulcrísimo – neat as a pin
Me muero de hambre. – I'm dying of hunger.

Q

que – what , that (conj.)
¡Qué lástima! – What a shame!
¡Qué lío! – What a drag!
Quedarse – to remain
querer (ie) – to want
querido/a – dear
el queso – cheese
quien – who
quince – fifteen
quinto (5to) – fifth

R

razón – right, justice
recibir – to receive
regresar – to return
relajar – to relax
el resfriado – cold, illness
el reventón – blow-out
robar – to steal
rojo/a – red
rosado/a – pink
el ruido – noise

S

sábado – Saturday
salir – to leave
¡Salud! – Cheers!
seguir (irreg.) – to follow
segundo (2do) – second
seis – six
Señor /Sr. – Sir or Mr.
Señora/Sra. Ma'am or Mrs.
Señorita /Srta. – Miss
sentarse – to sit
sentirse – to feel
septiembre – September
séptimo (7mo) – seventh
ser (irreg.) – to be
sesenta – sixty
setenta y uno – seventy-one
sexto (6to) – sixth
sí – yes
siete – seven
la silla – chair
simpático/a – nice
sin embargo – however
la sobrina – niece
el sobrino – nephew
¡Socorro! – Help!
el sol – sun
el sombrero – hat, headgear

la sopa – soup
sorprendentemente – surprisingly
sorprender – to surprise
el sostén – brassière
su/s – your (plural and polite); his/hers; their
suave – soft
subir – to climb up
la sudadera – sweatsuit
la suegra – mother-in-law
el suegro – father-in-law
el sueño – sleep
la suerte – luck
el suéter – sweater

T

tal vez – maybe
tamaño – huge
también – too
tarde – late
la tarde – afternoon
las tarjetas postales – postcards
te – to you (tú)
el té – tea
el teclado – keyboard
teclear – to type
temprano – early
tener (irreg.) – to have
tercero (3ro) – third
la tía – aunt
todavía – still
todo/a – every; all
tomar – to take
el tomate – tomato
la torta – cake
el trabajo – work
el trago – drink
el traje – suit
el traje de baño – bathing suit
trece – thirteen
treinta – thirty
treinta y uno – thirty-one
treinta y dos – thirty-two
el tren – the train
tres – three
triste – sad
tú – you, sing., fam.
tu/s – your (familiar)

U

un/una – a, masc./fem.
uno – one

usted/Ud. – you, sing., formal
ustedes/Uds. you, pl., formal

V

¡Vale! – OK!
valer(irreg.) – to be worth
veinte – twenty
veinticinco – twenty-five
veinticuatro – twenty-four
veintidós – twenty-two
veintinueve – twenty-nine
veintiocho – twenty-eight
veintiséis – twenty-six
veintisiete – twenty-seven
veintitrés – twenty-three
veintiuno – twenty-one
verde – green
las verduras – vegetables
el vestido – clothing
viajar – to travel
el viaje – trip
la vida – life
viejo/a – old
el viento – wind
viernes – Friday
el vino – wine
visitar – to visit
la vista – sight
vivir – to live
volver (ue) – to return
vosotros/as – you, plu., fam.

Y

y – and
yo – I
¡Yo también!/¡A mí también! – Me too!

Z

las zanahorias – carrots
los zapatos – shoes
los zapatos de tenis – tennis shoes

English-Spanish

A

a (masc./fem.) – un/una
a lot – mucho
A pleasure! ¡Mucho gusto!
afternoon – la tarde
afterward – después
again – otra vez
all – todo/a
almost – casi
also – también
amazing – asombroso
and – y
answering machine – la máquina contestadora
anyway – de todos modos
to appear – aparecer
appetizer – el antojito
apple – la manzana
April – abril
arm – el brazo
to ask – preguntarse
to ask for – pedir
at – a
at the crack of dawn – con el canto de los gallos
at the same time – a la vez
August – agosto
aunt – la tía
autumn – el otoño

B

back – la espalda
bad – mal
bakery – la panadería
bananas – las bananas
bathing suit – el traje de baño
bathroom – el baño
to be – estar
to be – ser (irreg.)
to be able – poderse
beans – los frijoles
beautiful – bello/a
bed – la cama
beer – la cerveza
to begin – empezar a
behind – detrás de
better – mejor
between – entre
beverage – la bebida
big – grande
black – negro
blouse – la blusa

blow-out – el reventón
blue – azul
body – el cuerpo
boots – las botas
bored – aburrido/a
boss – el jefe
both – por los dos (for)
bottle – la botella
box – la caja
boyfriend – el novio
brassière – el sostén
bread – el pan
to breakfast – desayunar
breakfast – el desayuno
bridge – el puente
to bring – llevar
brother – el hermano
brother-in-law – el cuñado
brown – marrón
buen(o) – good
business – el negocio
busy – ocupado/a
but – pero

C

cake – la torta
to be called – llamarse
candy – los dulces
car – el coche
cards – los naipes
carrots – las zanahorias
cat – el gato
celebrate – celebrar
celery – el apio
Certainly! – ¡Claro que sí!
chair – la silla
to charm – encantar
Cheers! – ¡Salud!
cheese – el queso
cherries – las cerezas
chest – el pecho
chestnut-colored – castaño
chicken – el pollo
city – la ciudad
clerk – el dependiente
to climb up – subir
close – íntimo
closed – cerrado/a
clothing – el vestido
coat – el abrigo
coconut – el coco
coffee – el café
cold – frío
cold, illness – el resfriado
to come – venir (ie)
to come to an end –

acabarse
comfortable – cómodo/a
computer programmer – el/la programador/a
to cook – cocinar
cook – el cocinero
countryside – el campo
to cross – cruzar

D

Darn! – ¡Caramba!
daughter – la hija
day – el día
day after tomorrow pasado mañana
day before yesterday – anteayer
dear – querido/a
December – diciembre
department store – el almacén
dessert – el postre
dinner – la cena
dog – el perro
domestic – casero/a
Don't mention it! – ¡No hay de que!
Don't worry? – ¡No te preocupes!
downstairs – abajo
dressing gown – la bata
drink – el trago
to drive – conducir

E

ear – la oreja
early – temprano
to eat – comer
eggs – los huevos
eight – ocho
eighteen – dieciocho
eighth – octavo (8vo)
eighty – ochenta
elbow – el codo
eleven – once
e-mail – el correo electrónico
English (lang.) – inglés
to enjoy – disfrutar
Enjoy your meal! – ¡Buen provecho!
enough – bastante
to enter – entrar
entertaining – divertido
even – aun
Excuse me! – ¡Perdón!
exhausted – agotado/a
eye – el ojo

F

facing – frente a
false – falso
far – lejos
father – el padre
father-in-law – el suegro
fear – el miedo
February – febrero
to feel – sentirse
fifteen – quince
fifth – quinto   (5to)
fifty – cincuenta
finger – el dedo
Fire! – ¡Incendio!
first – primero (1ro)
fish – el pescado
five – cinco
floor – el piso
flower(s) – la(s) flor(es)
to follow – seguir (irreg.)
food – la comida
foot – el pie
forty – cuarenta
four – cuatro
fourteen – catorce
fourth – cuarto (4to)
frankly – francamente
free – libre
French fries – las papas fritas
fresh – fresca
Friday – viernes
friend – el/la amigo/a
to frighten – dar miedo
fritters – los buñuelos
from/of – de
fruit – la fruta

G

to gain; to earn – ganar
garden – el jardín
to get – conseguir
to get lost – perderse
to get up – levantarse
girlfriend – la novia
to give – dar (irreg.)
glass – la copa
gloves – los guantes
to go – ir (irreg.)
to go bad – pasarse
to go; to walk – andar
good – bien
gourmet – epicúreo/a
granddaughter – la nieta
grandfather – el abuelo
grandmother – la abuela
grandson – el nieto

gray – gris
gray-haired – canoso
green – verde

H

half – media
ham – el jamón
hand – la mano
handsome – guapo/a
happy – contento/a
Happy Birthday! – ¡Feliz cumpleaños!
hat – el sombrero
he/ it, masculine – él
head – la cabeza
hello – hola
Help! – ¡Socorro!
here – aquí
highway – la carretera
his/hers – su/s
hot – calor
house – la casa
how – como
how much – cuanto
How much does it cost? – ¿Cuánto cuesta?
however – sin embargo
huge – tamaño
humid – húmedo
humorous – gracioso/a
hunger – hambre
to hurt – doler (ue)
husband – el esposo –

I

I – yo
I'm dying of hunger. – Me muero de hambre.
I don't care – me da iqual
I'm outta here. – Me voy.
I've had enough! – ¡Estoy harto!
ice cream – el helado
in fact – de hecho
in front of – enfrente de
in spite of – a pesar de
in, on – en
in my opinion – en mi opinión
in other words – en otras palabras
incredible – estupendo
inside – dentro de
it – lo/la
It was great! ¡Fue estupendo!

J

jacket – la chaqueta
January – enero
July – julio
June – junio

K

Keep your chin up! ¡Arriba los corazones!
keyboard – el teclado
to know – conocer

L

lake – el lago
last night – anoche
late – atrasados
late – tarde
to leave – salir
left – la izquierda
let's see – A ver
life – la vida
likewise – igualmente
line – la cola
little – poco
to live – vivir
long (length) – largo
love – el amor
luck – la suerte
lunch – almorzar (ue)
lunch – el almuerzo

M

Ma'am or Mrs. – Señora/ Sra.
to make/to do – hacer
man – el hombre
map – el mapa
March – marzo
to marry – casarse
May – mayo
maybe – tal vez
meat – la carne
Me too! – ¡Yo también! /¡A mí también!
to meet – encontrar(ue)
midnight – la medianoche
milk – la leche
Miss – Señorita /Srta.
Monday – lunes
month – el mes
more – más
morning – la mañana
mother – la madre
mother-in-law – la suegra
mouth – la boca

movies – el cine
mushrooms – los champiñones
my – mi/s
My goodness! – ¡Dios mío!

N

nearby – cerca de
neat as a pin – pulcrísimo/a
neck – el cuello
to need – necesitar
nephew – el sobrino
never – nunca
new – nuevo/a
next – el próximo
next to – al lado de
Never mind! – ¡No importa!
nice – amable
nice – simpático/a
niece – la sobrina
night – la noche
nine – nueve
nineteen – diecinueve
ninety – noventa
ninety-five – noventa y cinco
ninth – noveno (9no)
No way! – ¡De ninguna manera!
No way! – ¡No me digas!
noise – el ruido
none/nobody ningún/ninguna
noon – el mediodía
nose – la nariz
November – noviembre
now – ahora

O

to occupy – ocuparse
October – octubre
Of course not! ¡Claro que no!
Of course! – ¡Por supuesto!
often – a menudo
OK! – ¡Vale!
old – viejo/a
on sale – en venta
On the contrary! – ¡Al contrario!
on the other side of – al otro lado (de)
one – uno
one hundred – cien
one's own – propio/a

one-way – de ida
onion – la cebolla
open – abierto
orange – anaranjado/a
orange – la naranja
our – nuestro/a (os/as)
outdoors – al aire libre
outfit – la combinación
(de mujer)
outside – afuera
oven – el horno
owner – el dueño

P

pajamas – el pijama
pants – los pantalones
parents – los padres
park – el parque
party – la fiesta
to pass – pasar
past – pasado/a
pasta – los espaguetis
to pay – pagar
peas – los guisantes
pen – el bolígrafo
people – la gente
pie – el pastel
pink – rosado/a
plane – el avión
plate – el plato
to play (instrument) –
tocar
to play (sport) – jugar
(ue)
to please – gustar
please – por favor
Police! – ¡Policía!
poor – pobre
portable – portátil
postcards – las tarjetas
postales
to prefer – preferir (ie)
to present (oneself) –
presentarse
pretty – lindo/a
purse, handbag – la
bolsa
to put – poner

Q

quarter – cuarto
quick-tempered –
colérico/a

R

rain – la lluvia
to rain – llover
raincoat – el

impermeable
to read – leer
ready – listo/a
Really? – ¿De veras?
to receive – recibir
red – rojo/a
to relax – relajar
to remain – quedarse
to rent – alquilar
research – las
investigaciones
to return – regresar
to return – volver (ue)
rice – el arroz
right – el derecho
right. justice – razón
right now – ahorita
round-trip – de ida y
vuelta
rug – la alfombra
to run – correr

S

sad – triste
salad – la ensalada
same – mismo
Saturday – sábado
to say – decir (irreg.)
scarf – la bufanda
season – la estación
second – segundo (2do)
See you later! – ¡Hasta
luego!
to send – mandar
September – septiembre
seven – siete
seventeen – diecisiete
seventh – séptimo (7mo)
seventy-one – setenta
y uno
seventy-two – setenta
y dos
she/ it, feminine – ella
shoes – los zapatos
short – la camisa
short, length – corto/a
short, person – bajo/a
shorts – los pantalones
cortos
shoulder – el hombro
sick – enfermo/a
sight – la vista
Sir or Mr. – Señor /Sr.
sister – la hermana
to sit – sentarse
six – seis
sixteen – dieciséis
sixth – sexto (6to)
sixty – sesenta
to ski – esquiar

skirt – la falda
sleep – el sueño
to sleep – dormir (ue)
slippers – las pantuflas
slowly – lentamente
small – pequeño/a
snow – la nieve
to snow – nevar
so – así
socks – los calcetines
soft – suave
something – algo
son – el hijo
soon – pronto
soup – la sopa
Spanish (lang.) –
español
to speak – hablar
to spill – derramar
sport; game – el deporte
sports coat – la
chaqueta deportiva
stamps – las estampillas
star – la estrella
state – el estado
steak – el bistec
to steal – robar
still – todavía
stockings – las medias
stomach – el estómago
to stop – parar
to stop (motoring) –
pararse
strawberries – las fresas
street – la calle
stylish – de moda
suit – el traje
suitcase – la maleta
summer – el verano
sun – el sol
Sunday – domingo
surf the Web – navegar
la red
to surprise – sorprender
surprisingly –
sorprendentemente
swamped –
atareadísimo/a
sweater – el suéter
sweatsuit – la sudadera
sweet roll, bun – el pan
dulce
to swim – nadar

T

to take – tomar
tall, person – alto/a
tea – el té
teeth – los dientes

to telephone – llamar
ten – diez
tennis shoes – los
zapatos de tenis
tenth – décimo (10mo)
to test – probar (ue)
thanks – gracias
that – ese/a
that (thing) over there
(neuter) – aquello
that (thing, neuter) –
eso
that one – ése/a
that one over there –
aquél/la
that over there – aquel/
la
That's cool! – ¡Chévere!
That's enough! – ¡Basta!
the, feminine – la
the, masculine – el
their – su/s
then – entonces
there is/there are – hay
there, (over) – allá
these – estos/as
these ones – éstos/as
they, feminine – ellas
they, masculine – ellos
Thief! – ¡Ladrón!
to think – creer
to think – pensar (ie)
third – tercero (3ro)
thirteen – trece
thirty – treinta
thirty-one – treinta y
uno
thirty-two – treinta y
dos
this – este/a
this (thing, neuter) –
esto
this one – éste/a
those – esos/as
those ones – ésos/as
those ones over there –
aquéllos/as
those over there –
aquellos/as
three – tres
Thursday – jueves
ticket – el billete
ticket – el boleto
tie, neck/bowtie – la
corbata
time – la hora
tired – cansado/a
to him/her/it/you (Ud.)
to me – me
to them/you (Uds.) – les
to us – nos

to y'all (vosotros) – os
to you (tú) – te
today – hoy
toes – los dedos del pie
together – junto/a
tomato – el tomate
tomorrow – mañana
ton – el montón – a
too (much) – demasiado
toys – los juguetes
track – andén
train – el tren
to travel – caminar
to travel – viajar
trip – el viaje
throat – la garganta
true – cierto
truth – la verdad
to try out – ensayar
Tuesday – martes
to turn on – encenderse (ie)
twelve – doce
twenty – veinte
twenty-eight – veintiocho
twenty-five – veinticinco
twenty-four – veinticuatro
twenty-nine – veintinueve
twenty-one – veintiuno
twenty-seven – veintisiete
twenty-six – veintiséis
twenty-three – veintitrés
twenty-two – veintidós
two – dos
to type – teclear

U

U.S.A. – los estados unidos
umbrella – el paraguas
uncle – el tío
underneath – debajo/a
underpants – los calzoncillos
undershirt – la camiseta
to understand – comprender
unfortunately – desafortunadamente
upstairs – arriba

V

vegetables – las verduras
very – muy

to visit – visitar

W

to wake up – despertarse
walk – el paseo
to want – querer (ie
to wash (oneself) – lavarse
to watch – mirar
water – la agua
we – nosotros/as
weather – el tiempo
Wednesday – miércoles
weekend – el fin de semana
weight – el peso
what – que
What a drag! – ¡Qué lío!
What a shame! – ¡Qué lástima!
when – cuando
where – dónde
while – mientras
white – blanco/a
wife – la esposa
window – la ventana
windy – viento
wine – el vino
winter – el invierno
with me – conmigo
woman – la mujer
wood(s); forest – el bosque
work – el trabajo
Wow! – ¡Ay!

Y

year – el año
to yell – gritar
yellow – amarillo/a
yes – sí
yesterday – ayer
you (plu., fam.) – vosotros/as
you (plu., for.) – ustedes/Uds.
you (sing., fam.) – tú
you (sing., for.) – usted/Ud.
You're kidding! – ¡Me estás bromeando!
you're welcome – de nada
young – joven
your (familiar) – tu/s
your (plural and polite) – su/s

Z

zero – cero

SPAIN

La Religión en Países Hispanos

The majority of people living in Spanish-speaking countries is Catholic. The influence of religion can be seen in many aspects of Hispanic culture, from family life to art. Sunday is a day for church, friends and family. Many churches are located in the "plaza mayor" (town square), a situation that encourages socializing and interacting within the community. Numerous local events and celebrations are centered around the church and its congregation.

Religious holidays are very important as well, and many fascinating traditions are associated with them. One example is Holy Week, known as Semana Santa, the week between Palm Sunday (el Domingo de Ramos) and Easter (la Pascua). Many people have a week of vacation from work at this time. Celebrations during Semana Santa vary among different countries, but often include elaborate floral decorations and processions or parades. Seville, Spain (Sevilla) is one city that's famous for its Semana Santa celebrations. Semana Santa is a great time to visit a Spanish-speaking country!

Spanish explorers and conquistadores brought the Spanish tradition of Catholicism to the New World. Spanish clergy attempted to convert as many Native Americans as possible to Catholicism; many of the native people took up some practices of the Catholic Church while disregarding others. The result of this process after a couple of centuries is a somewhat altered version of the Catholic religion; the traditions of Catholicism have become interwoven with those of the Pre-Columbian religions practiced in Latin America. One excellent example of this mingling of traditions is the observation of "el Día de los Santos" and "el Día de los Muertos" (common to Mexico and some Hispanic communities in the US.) These important religious holidays are a combination of the Catholic All Saints & All Souls Days with the Pre-Columbian festival days in celebration of the harvest.

"Los Días de los Muertos" are celebrated on the 1st and 2nd of November. It is believed that the souls of the departed visit the living during these days. "El Día de los Santos", celebrated on November 1st, is a day particularly in memory of children who have died. "El Día de los Muertos", on the 2nd of November, is for remembering all loved ones who have passed on. These are very important and widely observed holidays in most of Latin America; a lot of work goes into preparing for them. Each family creates an altar in memory of the dearly departed, featuring some of his or her favorite things, particularly food and beverages the dead person enjoyed while living.

In addition to preparing and savoring a rich variety of foods, many Mexicans create wonderful artwork to commemorate los Días de los Muertos. Sometimes the art is edible! Designs featuring skeletons and skulls take many forms; papier-maché figures and puppets portray skeletons engaged in various everyday activities, often playing musical instruments. Many of the altars created for los Días de los Muertos incorporate such figures and are quite artistic and elaborate. Parades feature people dressed in scary or silly costumes who dance or act out darkly comedic vignettes related to death and dying. Many of the traditional foods eaten during this time have similar themes. Sugar skulls and other skull or skeleton-shaped cakes and candies are very popular, and the typical "pan de muertos" is decorated on top with pieces of bread shaped to resemble bones.

Although there are somber moments during these days, the general mood is festive. All ages can enjoy the culinary treats, parades and festive decorations. Popular decorations include paper cutouts, colorful gourds and fruits, and an abundance of flowers and candles. Many families take floral arrangements and other items to the cemetery to decorate the graves of loved ones. Marigolds are everywhere; the Marigold is known as "la flor de muertos" and is traditionally associated with los Días de los Muertos. The traditional festive celebrations marking these days portray death as something familiar, a part of everyday life rather than a fearsome unknown. Such an attitude toward death and the afterlife is a direct result of the influence of indigenous beliefs and rituals on the Catholic religious traditions imported from Spain.

Of course, different regions throughout the Spanish-speaking world have their own special ways of commemorating religious (and political) holidays, flavored by local traditions. If you're lucky enough to be in town for any kind of special celebration or festival, you're sure to enjoy it!

¡Vamos a comer!

Some interesting differences exist between the eating habits customary in Hispanic countries and those you may be familiar with. As you might expect, many of the foods commonly eaten will be different. In addition, the timing and relative size of daily meals in Spanish-speaking countries and the nature of "eating out" are unlike the same practices in much of the English-speaking world.

In general, meals are eaten somewhat later in the day in Spanish-speaking countries than they are in many English-speaking countries. Breakfast, for example, is often eaten around 8:00–10:00 am in much of the Hispanic world. It tends to be a light meal, usually featuring bread or rolls with butter and jam, coffee or hot chocolate. It is much less common for people to eat eggs or meats at breakfast.

While many English-speaking people eat more at dinner than at other meals of the day, in many parts of the Spanish-speaking world lunch is the largest meal of the day. It is usually consumed sometime

between 2:00 and 4:00 in the afternoon; most businesses close for a couple of hours around the same time while the employees enjoy a leisurely lunch, often at home with other family members. Lunch generally consists of two courses plus dessert and wine. A typical lunch for someone living in a Spanish-speaking country might be grilled fish or chicken with rice or potatoes, a mixed salad and flan or fruit for dessert. Don't forget to look for local specialties, such as mixed grill in Argentina, tamales in Mexico, or filled "arepas" (a round, fried bread) in Venezuela. In Spain, sampling the local paella (a rice dish with saffron, vegetables and seafood) is a must!

Dinner is also eaten fairly late. Many restaurants do not even start serving dinner until 9 o'clock at night. This is particularly true in Spain, where it is the custom to enjoy some wine or Sangría with a variety of snacks known collectively as "tapas" at around 7 or 8 in the evening. Many bars offer a selection of delicious choices from which you'll request portions (just the right size for snacking) of your favorites. There's sure to be something you'll like! "Tapas" are often substantial snacks such as bits of specialty ham or sausage, mushrooms or potatoes in garlic sauce, shrimp (called "gambas" in Spain) and of course "tortilla", which in Spain refers to an egg dish similar to an omelet with potatoes and onions. Some offerings are more exotic! Be adventurous and try as many as you can.

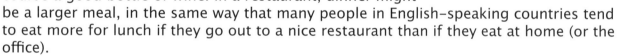

After such a substantial snack, it's no wonder people don't get hungry for dinner until maybe 10:00 or later. When they get around to eating it, dinner can be a fairly light meal. Some eggs with bread and cheese might be a tasty dinner, or perhaps fried potatoes and sausages...and of course a good bottle of wine. In a restaurant, dinner might be a larger meal, in the same way that many people in English-speaking countries tend to eat more for lunch if they go out to a nice restaurant than if they eat at home (or the office).

What about fast food, which is so popular in North America? If you visit a larger metropolitan area, you're likely to see a few familiar fast food chains. They may offer some different food choices, but overall they're pretty much what you'd expect. However, fast food is not nearly as popular in Spanish-speaking countries as it is in the United States. Drive-through windows are much less common, and ordering food "to go" is more the exception than the rule. If people do go to a "fast-food" restaurant, they most often sit down in the restaurant to eat their food rather than getting it "to go". You will rarely see someone eating a burger or drinking coffee while driving, as is so common in the United States! Home delivery from a restaurant is also rare – only a few large pizza chains offer this service to very limited areas. Another difference that might be unexpected to you is that the menu items at fast-food restaurants tend to be on the expensive side compared to other possible food choices; thus for many it is an occasional indulgence but too expensive to eat frequently.

Fast food fits much better into North American "fast culture" than into the pace of life in Hispanic countries. For people living in Spanish-speaking countries, eating is one of life's important pleasures, to be savored and enjoyed with loved ones in a congenial setting.

The company and conversation are at least as important as the food and wine. After a nice lunch, you might see people lingering at a sidewalk café, sipping coffee and enjoying the scenery. One feature of the more relaxed lifestyle in most Hispanic countries is that bringing a client the bill (la cuenta) without being asked is considered very rude! Be aware of this, and signal the waiter (or waitress) when you'd like to pay the bill. Otherwise, you may sit waiting for quite awhile.

What about the tip (la propina)? When you get your bill, it's likely that a 10% tip (usually denoted as "servicio") will have already been added. (This is a very common practice throughout the Spanish–speaking world.) If you were especially pleased with the service, feel free to leave something extra; most people leave whatever smaller coins they get back as change from the bill for their server.

Food is an important part of any culture! Try different kinds of restaurants, cafés, and if you are adventurous, roadside stands and kiosks. Find out what the local specialties are and sample them! Of course, a great way to experience the local cuisine is to dine in someone's home. If you are lucky enough to be invited to someone's house for dinner, bring a bottle of wine and prepare to enjoy a wonderful meal!

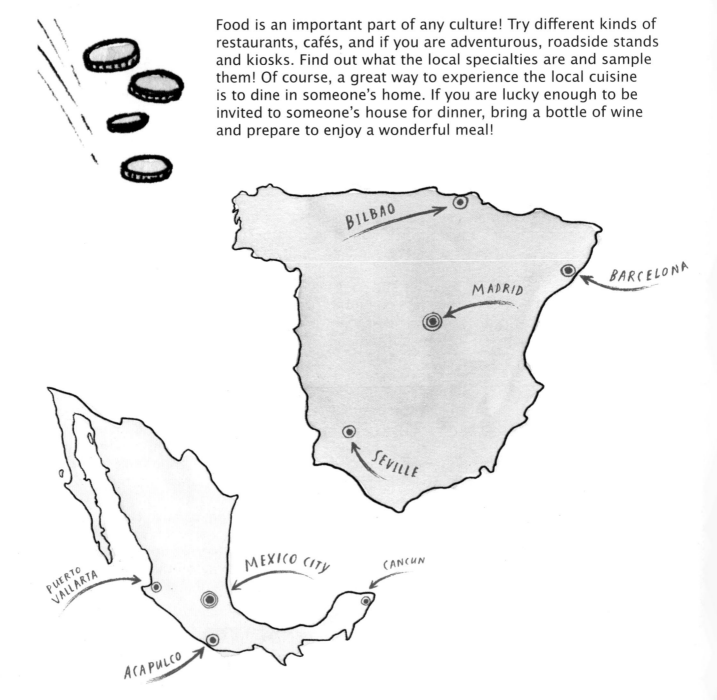

Paste these removable stickers around your work and home.
It will re-enforce what you've learned!

(keh oRROR)
¡Qué horror!

(mehHOR TARdeh keh NOONka)
¡Mejor tarde que nunca!

(aSEE ehs la BEEtha)
¡Así es la vida!

(bwehn BYAheh)
¡Buen viaje!

(keh paSO)
¿Qué pasó?

(soKOrro)
¡Socorro!

(eenSEHNdyo)
¡Incendio!

(DOHNdeh ehsTA la ehmbaHAda ehsTAdoh-ooneeDEHNseh)
¿Dónde está la embajada estadounidense?

(Ehso teh KEHda mooy byehn)
¡Eso te queda muy bien!

(deh neenGOOna maNEHra)
¡De ninguna manera!

(no teh preoKOOpehs)
¡No te preocupes!

(keh teh Pasa)
¿Qué te pasa?

(ehsTOY agoTAdoh)
Estoy agotado.

(ehsTOY atareaDEEseema)
Estoy atareadísima.

(saLOOTH)
¡Salud!

(bwehn proBEHcho)
¡Buen provecho!

(keh LEEo)
¡Qué lío!

(meh boy)
Me voy.

(esTAS bromehANdoh)
¡Estás bromeando!

(ehsTOY ARtoh)
¡Estoy harto!

(fweh ehstooPEHNdoh)
¡Fue estupendo!

(no meh DEEgas)
¡No me digas!

(kaRAHMba)
¡Caramba!

(kohn MOOcho GOOStoh)
¡Con mucho gusto!

(CHEHbehreh)
Chévere.

(BAHSta)
¡Basta!

(KOmo)
¿Cómo?

(BAHmos ah behr)
Vamos a ver...

(aRREEba los koraZOnehs)
¡Arriba los corazones!

(no eemPORta)
¡No importa!

(AHSta LWEHgo)
¡Hasta luego!

(BAHleh)
¡Vale!

(no ay deh keh)
No hay de que.

(keh SWEHRteh)
¡Qué suerte!

(pehrDOHN)
¡Perdón!

(TEHNgo SWEHnyo)
Tengo sueño.

(TEHNgo seth)
Tengo sed,

(TEHNgo AHMbreh)
Tengo hambre.

(meh da iGWAL)
Me da igual

(BAmos)
Vamos.